the **Homes** *of* **Carmichael** *and* **Dame**™
volume two

CDD

Publisher	Dennis Brozak
Associate Publisher	Linda Reimer
Editor	Kevin Blair
Plans Editor	Tina Leyden
Designer	Robert Dame
Writer	Carol Stratman Shea
Rendering Illustrator	Sylvia Boyd
Graphic Artists	Yen Gutowski
	Heather Guthrie
	Jeff Dedlow
	Mary Fitzmaurice
Production Assistant	Jeff Blair
Technical Advisors	Patrick Carmichael
	Pat Berrios
	Carl Cuozzo
	Rob Phillips
Circulation Manager	Priscilla Ivey

The Homes of Carmichael & Dame™ Volume II
is published by:
Design Basics Publications
11112 John Galt Blvd., Omaha, NE 68137
WEB – www.designbasics.com
E-MAIL – info@designbasics.com

CEO	Dennis Brozak
President	Linda Reimer
Marketing Director	Kevin Blair
Business Development	Paul Foresman
Controller	Janie Murnane
Editor-in-Chief	Bruce Arant

Printed in Hong Kong through Palace Press International
Text and Design © 2000 by Design Basics Inc.
Plans © 1999 by Carmichael & Dame
All rights reserved.

No part of this publication may be reproduced in any
form or by any means without prior written permission
of the publisher.

HOME PLAN DESIGN SERVICE

Library of Congress No. 99-075874
ISBN: 1-892150-17-4

Patrick Carmichael and Robert Dame

*F*or more than a decade, Carmichael & Dame designs have decorated the landscape with the brilliance and elegance of luxury home plans. Both Patrick Carmichael and Robert Dame started out as building contractors before joining together in 1987 as the design-build firm, Carmichael & Dame.

It was not long before they were recognized as one of the top building and design firms in their hometown of Houston, Texas. They received recognition for their work in both design and business, including BUILDER Magazine's America's Best Builder Award, Houston's Prism Award for Custom Home of the Year and the National Quality Housing Award. In 1996, they designed and built the New American Home™ showcased at the NAHB's Annual Builders' Show.

Today the team concentrates exclusively on developing innovative design for clientele nationwide. The design team is led by Robert Dame, whose unique design style paved the way for the release of their Timeless Legacy Collection. This second volume is an exciting extension of their work over the past six years, featuring many popular, previously released designs, along with many brand-new designs.

When artists create a painting or sculpture, it has to excite the eye, or the touch. In contrast, homes not only have to be pleasing esthetically, but they also have to breathe and function. A home has to be durable, easy to live in and have the ability to grow with a family. It has to withstand the elements. The design of a home is art entwined with function.

This philosophy is the way designer Robert Dame views his work. The 50 new designs in this latest collection from Carmichael & Dame represent the delicate marriage of function and form. The designs themselves are distinguishable the moment they are studied, for one sees recurring themes – no two ever alike – in a wide variety of styles and square footages.

The exterior beauty of these homes is apparent. All elevations were carefully crafted to allow enjoyment regardless of the vantage point from which they are viewed. This allows a less rigid front-to-back positioning on a home site.

Likewise, the interior of each home is an individual experience. Each space is spontaneous in its location and appeal. Family areas are often decidedly open, lending themselves to a more casual atmosphere. All the homes, whether modest or mansion-like in square footage, can function and adapt according to the lifestyle of the homeowners.

It is clear that light and views are important, as this collection reveals in open living spaces and elegant stair towers. Two-story rooms bring light and views from two levels and allow enjoyment and celebration from many angles.

Exterior living spaces are carefully integrated with interior areas to suggest connection when entertaining or relaxing. They are spacious, allowing a variety of furnishings to create comfortable living outdoor spaces. As a result, many can be enclosed or screened in for additional living space tied to the home.

Function is clearly important, though often hidden behind these homes' more esthetic elements. Dame carefully considered each room for furniture placement and entertainment pieces – many of which are built in for convenience.

Each garage was designed for ease in adaptation from front-load to side-load. Many easily convert from two-car to three-car accommodations. Others can function as detached garages without affecting the design of the home.

The marriage of function and form is part of what separates architecture from art. Carmichael & Dame designs represent a unique interpretation of that marriage in the form of surprising light sources, outdoor living spaces and continuity of interior rooms. This is what separates Carmichael & Dame from all other designers and what will ultimately stand the test of time.

——————— CDD ———————

*I*n studying the designs on the following pages, one sees the true advantages of a one-story. Designer Robert Dame has given careful thought to the placement of bedrooms, often splitting the master suite from the secondary bedrooms. The family room is the hub of all his one-story homes, surrounded by an easy placement of rooms, designed with a natural traffic flow. Though one-story homes aren't often known for their outdoor living spaces, nearly all of these designs feature porches or verandas – whether on the front or rear of the home. These one-story homes are noted for their ability to adapt to individual needs, particularly through the variety of flexible rooms. Home offices are often positioned near full baths, for use as a bedroom, and upper-level attic space can be utilized for storage or future expansion.

One-Story **Homes**

Creekbend Manor

*B*ayed windows in the breakfast room allow a unique vantage point from which to view those entering the home. • Deliberately separate from two additional bedrooms, the master suite adjoins the rear porch and offers a bath with individual vanities, a whirlpool tub and walk-in closet with built-ins and natural light.

PLAN 9187-9R

price code 17

Call toll-free
800-947-7526
www.designbasics.com

Total Living Area   1751 Sq. Ft.

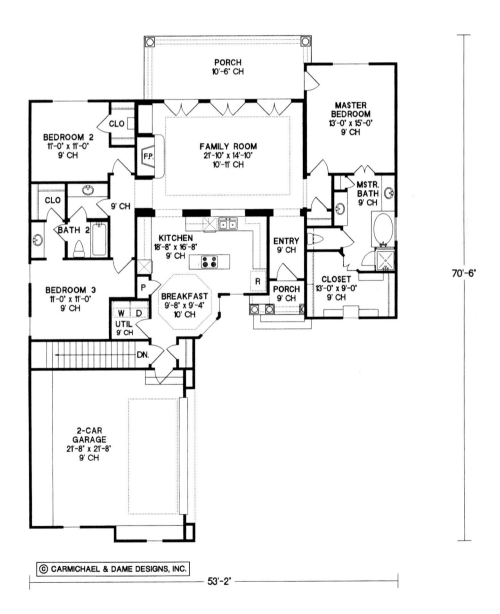

PORCH
10'-6" CH

MASTER
BEDROOM
13'-0" x 15'-0"
9' CH

CLO

BEDROOM 2
11'-0" x 11'-0"
9' CH

F.P.

FAMILY ROOM
21'-10" x 14'-10"
10'-11' CH

MSTR.
BATH
9' CH

CLO

9' CH

BATH 2

KITCHEN
18'-8' x 16'-8'
9' CH

ENTRY
9' CH

BEDROOM 3
11'-0" x 11'-0"
9' CH

P

R

CLOSET
13'-0" x 9'-0"
9' CH

BREAKFAST
9'-8' x 9'-4'
10' CH

PORCH
9' CH

W   D

UTIL
9' CH

DN.

70'-6"

2-CAR
GARAGE
21'-8' x 21'-8'
9' CH

53'-2"

© CARMICHAEL & DAME DESIGNS, INC.

7

Windrush Estate

A front porch on this sprawling one-story leads inside, where the view passes through the family room and onto the rear porch. • A long, island counter seats the whole family for breakfast. • An organized master closet features a window and is steps from the bath with whirlpool tub, double vanity and linen cabinet.

PLAN 9198-9R

price code 18

Call toll-free
800-947-7526
www.designbasics.com

CUSTOMIZE
any home plan

Total Living Area   1876 Sq. Ft.

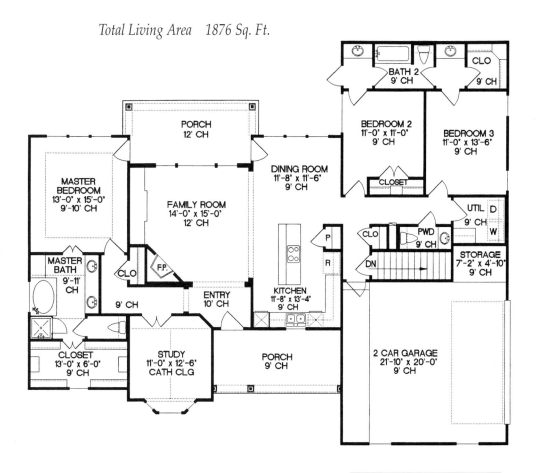

PORCH
12' CH

BATH 2
9' CH

CLO
9' CH

BEDROOM 2
11'-0" x 11'-0"
9' CH

BEDROOM 3
11'-0" x 13'-6"
9' CH

MASTER
BEDROOM
13'-0" x 15'-0"
9'-10" CH

DINING ROOM
11'-8" x 11'-6"
9' CH

FAMILY ROOM
14'-0" x 15'-0"
12' CH

CLOSET

UTIL   D
9' CH
W

MASTER
BATH
9'-11"
CH

CLO

F.P.

9' CH

CLO

PWD
9' CH

STORAGE
7'-2" x 4'-10"
9' CH

P

DN

CLOSET
13'-0" x 6'-0"
9' CH

STUDY
11'-0" x 12'-6"
CATH CLG

ENTRY
10' CH

KITCHEN
11'-8" x 13'-4"
9' CH

R

PORCH
9' CH

2 CAR GARAGE
21'-10" x 20'-0"
9' CH

52'-8"

65'-0"

© CARMICHAEL & DAME DESIGNS, INC.

Waterside Estate

*T*he subtly arched front porch on this home is elegantly combined with copper accents and a double gable garage. • Inside, a study easily converts into a dining room, and is steps from the kitchen. • Counters curve to bring definition to the kitchen, which offers an island and walk-in pantry. • An eight-sided family room joins with the rear porch through a set of French doors.

PLAN 9201-9R
price code 19

Call toll-free
800-947-7526
www.designbasics.com

Total Living Area   1926 Sq. Ft.

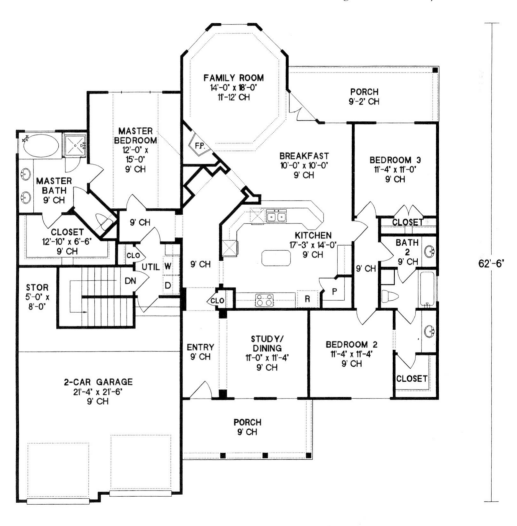

© CARMICHAEL & DAME DESIGNS, INC.

Westcott Manor

$\mathcal{L}$ap siding and a copper-trimmed roof give refreshing appeal to this one-story home. • The master suite is separated from two other bedrooms and is an ideal place to relax on a rear porch or in a bath behind French doors. • Second-level attic space makes this home easily expandable.

Call toll-free
800-947-7526
www.designbasics.com

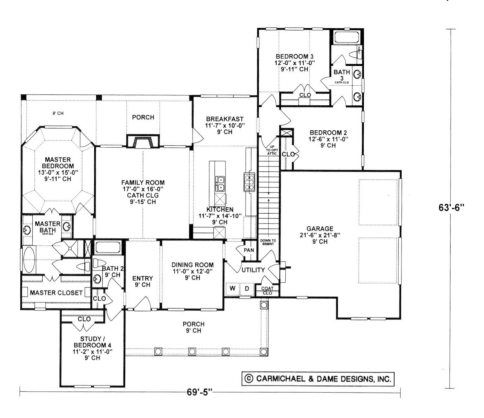

Master Bedroom 13'-0" x 15'-0" 9'-11" CH

9' CH

PORCH

BREAKFAST 11'-7" x 10'-0" 9' CH

BEDROOM 3 12'-0" x 11'-0" 9'-11" CH

BATH 3 CATH CLG

CLO

FAMILY ROOM 17'-0" x 16'-0" CATH CLG 9'-15' CH

KITCHEN 11'-7" x 14'-10" 9' CH

UP TO OPT ATTIC

CLO

BEDROOM 2 12'-6" x 11'-0" 9' CH

MASTER BATH CATH CLG

DOWN TO BSMNT

GARAGE 21'-6" x 21'-8" 9' CH

BATH 2 9' CH

DINING ROOM 11'-0" x 12'-0" 9' CH

PAN

UTILITY

63'-6"

MASTER CLOSET

ENTRY 9' CH

W D

COAT CLO

CLO

CLO

PORCH 9' CH

STUDY / BEDROOM 4 11'-2" x 11'-0" 9' CH

© CARMICHAEL & DAME DESIGNS, INC.

69'-5"

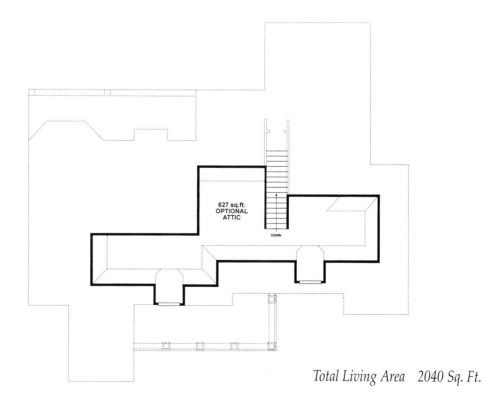

627 sq.ft. OPTIONAL ATTIC

DOWN

Total Living Area   2040 Sq. Ft.

Winston Court

*T*he beauty of this home's stone and siding exterior hides its functional interior layout that offers a variety of shared vistas. • Arches frame the entry into the study, which catches views of a rear porch and breakfast room. • By opening four sets of French doors, the porch becomes an integrated part of the main living areas.

Call toll-free
800-947-7526
www.designbasics.com

PLAN 9206-9R
price code 22

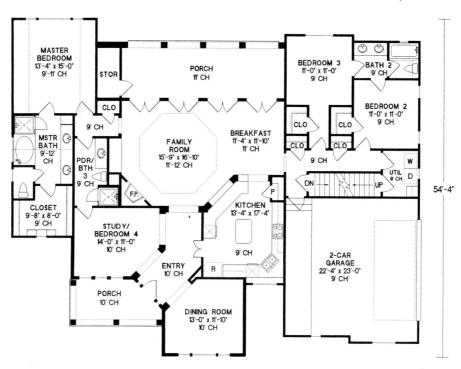

MASTER BEDROOM
13'-4" x 15'-0"
9'-11' CH

STOR

PORCH
11' CH

BEDROOM 3
11'-0" x 11'-0"
9' CH

BATH 2
9' CH

CLO

BEDROOM 2
11'-0" x 11'-0"
9' CH

MSTR BATH
9'-12'
CH

PDR/ BTH 3
9' CH

FAMILY ROOM
15'-9" x 16'-10"
11'-12' CH

BREAKFAST
11'-4" x 11'-10"
11' CH

CLO

CLO

CLO

CLO

9' CH

W

D

UTIL
9' CH

CLOSET
9'-8" x 8'-0"
9' CH

F.P.

STUDY/ BEDROOM 4
14'-0" x 11'-0"
10' CH

P

DN

UP

9' CH

KITCHEN
13'-4" x 17'-4"

ENTRY
10' CH

R

9' CH

2-CAR GARAGE
22'-4" x 23'-0"
9' CH

PORCH
10' CH

DINING ROOM
13'-0" x 11'-10"
10' CH

54'-4"

© CARMICHAEL & DAME DESIGNS, INC.

68'-0"

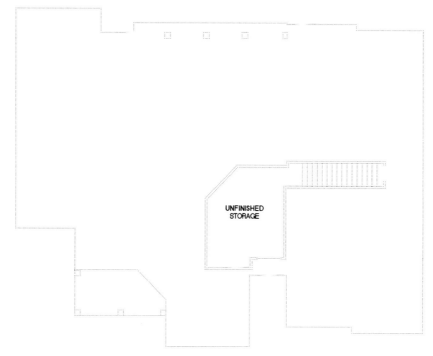

UNFINISHED STORAGE

Total Living Area   2203 Sq. Ft.

Longworth Estate

*T*hree sets of double doors attach themselves to the front, wrap-around veranda. • The kitchen features a walk-in pantry, island counter and snack bar. • A bath with split vanities serves three bedrooms in a segregated wing that secludes the master suite to a rear corner.

Call toll-free
800-947-7526
www.designbasics.com

PLAN 9185-9R
price code 22

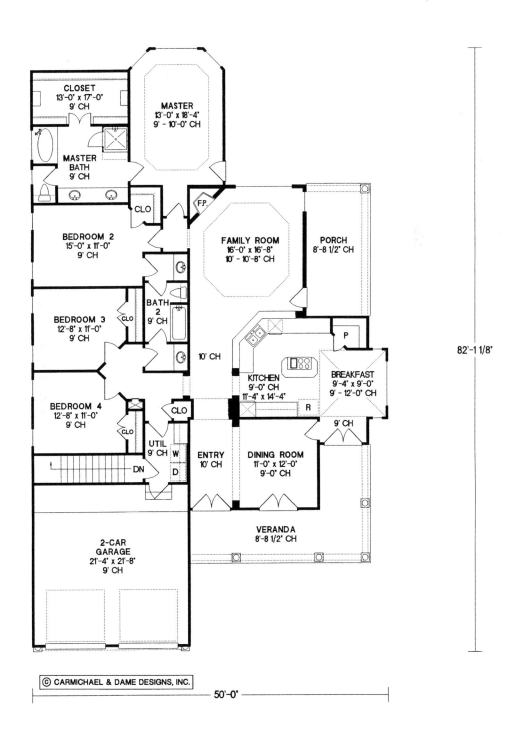

CLOSET
13'-0" x 17'-0"
9' CH

MASTER
13'-0" x 18'-4"
9' - 10'-0" CH

MASTER
BATH
9' CH

CLO

F.P.

FAMILY ROOM
16'-0" x 16'-8"
10' - 10'-8" CH

PORCH
8'-8 1/2" CH

BEDROOM 2
15'-0" x 11'-0"
9' CH

BATH
2
9' CH

BEDROOM 3
12'-8" x 11'-0"
9' CH

CLO

10' CH

KITCHEN
9'-0" CH
11'-4" x 14'-4"

P

BREAKFAST
9'-4" x 9'-0"
9' - 12'-0" CH

R

9' CH

BEDROOM 4
12'-8" x 11'-0"
9' CH

CLO

CLO

UTIL
9' CH

W

D

ENTRY
10' CH

DINING ROOM
11'-0" x 12'-0"
9'-0" CH

DN

2-CAR
GARAGE
21'-4" x 21'-8"
9' CH

VERANDA
8'-8 1/2" CH

82'-1 1/8"

50'-0"

© CARMICHAEL & DAME DESIGNS, INC.

Total Living Area   2211 Sq. Ft.

Alexander Court

*T*he rear porch on this home is divided into three visual segments. • A sloped ceiling in the family room extends onto the central portion for interest. • French doors in the master suite open onto another segment, while the breakfast area enjoys its own portion, which provides a place for a meal in the fresh air.

PLAN 9189-9R

price code 22

Call toll-free
800-947-7526
www.designbasics.com

Total Living Area 2256 Sq. Ft.

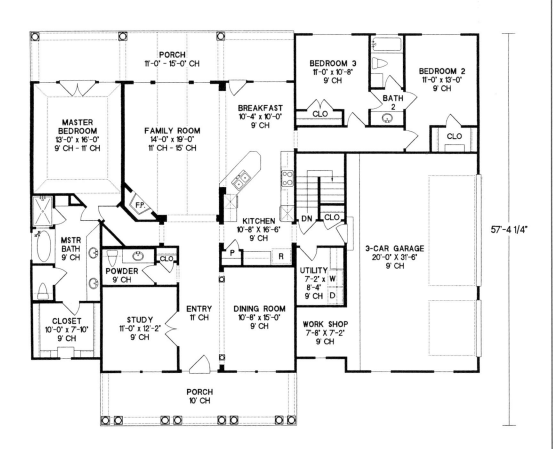

© CARMICHAEL & DAME DESIGNS, INC.

Briar Manor

*T*his charming home is characterized by its separated garages, offering a place for storage or a classic automobile. • The dining room, easily converted into a living room, is the central focus upon entry. • Its fireplace and rear windows will inspire relaxation. • The informal family room is equally exciting with a vaulted ceiling and second hearth.

PLAN 9207-9R

price code 23

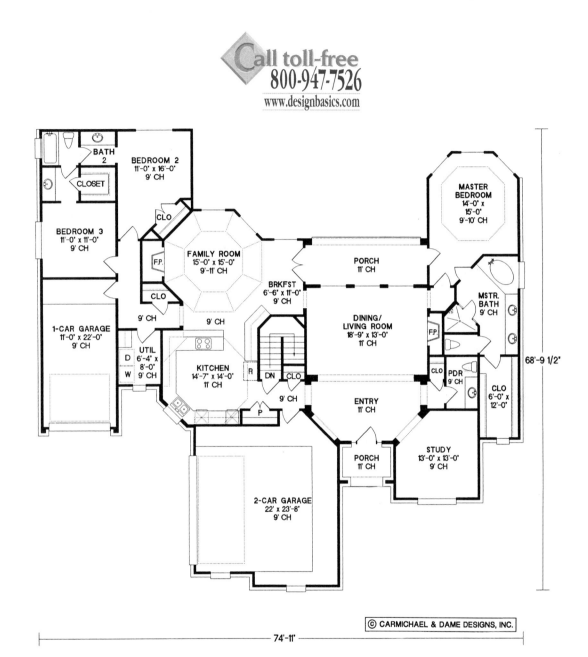

Call toll-free
800-947-7526
www.designbasics.com

BATH 2

BEDROOM 2
11'-0" x 16'-0"
9' CH

CLOSET

BEDROOM 3
11'-0" x 11'-0"
9' CH

CLO

CLO

FAMILY ROOM
15'-0" x 15'-0"
9'-11' CH

F.P.

CLO

MASTER BEDROOM
14'-0" x 15'-0"
9'-10' CH

PORCH
11' CH

BRKFST
6'-6" x 11'-0"
9' CH

MSTR. BATH
9' CH

1-CAR GARAGE
11'-0" x 22'-0"
9' CH

9' CH

9' CH

DINING/ LIVING ROOM
18'-9" x 13'-0"
11' CH

F.P.

D

UTIL
6'-4" x 8'-0"
9' CH

W

KITCHEN
14'-7" x 14'-0"
11' CH

DN

CLO

R

CLO

PDR
9' CH

CLO
6'-0" x 12'-0"

68'-9 1/2"

P

9' CH

ENTRY
11' CH

2-CAR GARAGE
22' x 23'-8"
9' CH

PORCH
11' CH

STUDY
13'-0" x 13'-0"
9' CH

© CARMICHAEL & DAME DESIGNS, INC.

— 74'-11" —

Total Living Area   2331 Sq. Ft.

ORIGINAL DRAFT
ALL PLANS HAVE BEEN REGISTERED
WITH THE U.S. COPYRIGHT OFFICE

21

The front porch grants access into the entry and dining room, both of which enjoy a view of a central see-through fireplace. • In the kitchen, a long, eating bar seats the whole family for breakfast. • The study converts to a guest suite with secluded access.

Call toll-free
800-947-7526
www.designbasics.com

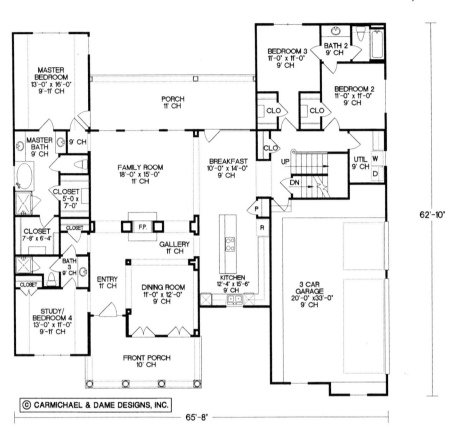

MASTER
BEDROOM
13'-0" x 16'-0"
9'-11" CH

PORCH
11' CH

BEDROOM 3
11'-0" x 11'-0"
9' CH

BATH 2
9' CH

BEDROOM 2
11'-0" x 11'-0"
9' CH

MASTER
BATH
9' CH

9' CH

CLO

CLO

FAMILY ROOM
18'-0" x 15'-0"
11' CH

CLOSET
5'-0 x
7'-0"

CLOSET

CLOSET
7'-8" x 6'-4"

F.P.

GALLERY
11' CH

BREAKFAST
10'-0" x 14'-0"
9' CH

CLO

UP

DN

UTIL
9' CH

W
D

P

R

BATH
3
9' CH

CLOSET

ENTRY
11' CH

DINING ROOM
11'-0" x 12'-0"
9' CH

KITCHEN
12'-4" x 15'-6"
9' CH

3 CAR
GARAGE
20'-0" x 33'-0"
9' CH

STUDY/
BEDROOM 4
13'-0" x 11'-0"
9'-11" CH

FRONT PORCH
10' CH

© CARMICHAEL & DAME DESIGNS, INC.

65'-8"

62'-10"

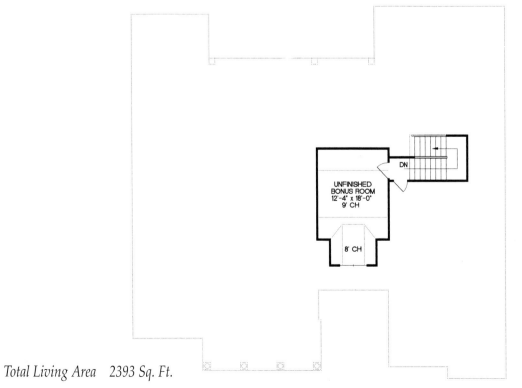

UNFINISHED
BONUS ROOM
12'-4" x 18'-0"
9' CH

DN

8' CH

Total Living Area   2393 Sq. Ft.

Unfinished Future Space adds 222 Sq. Ft.

Edgewater Court

$\mathscr{A}$ central corridor in this home produces views from the entry to the rear and between the dining room and family room. • A rear porch is an important element, accessible from the master suite and breakfast area. • The kitchen is highly functional, with a peninsula snack bar, walk-in pantry and service counter near the dining room.

PLAN 9159-9R
price code 24

Call toll-free
800-947-7526
www.designbasics.com

Total Living Area   2409 Sq. Ft.

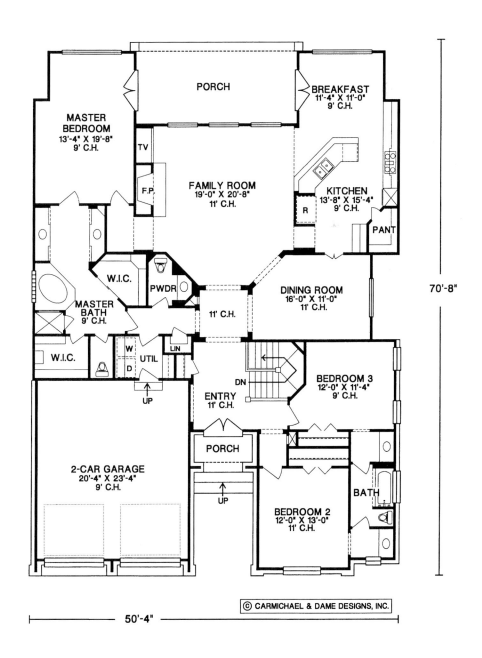

PORCH

MASTER BEDROOM
13'-4" X 19'-8"
9' C.H.

BREAKFAST
11'-4" X 11'-0"
9' C.H.

TV

F.P.

FAMILY ROOM
19'-0" X 20'-8"
11' C.H.

KITCHEN
13'-8" X 15'-4"
9' C.H.

R

PANT

W.I.C.

PWDR

MASTER BATH
9' C.H.

11' C.H.

DINING ROOM
16'-0" X 11'-0"
11' C.H.

W.I.C.

W
D

UTIL

LIN

DN

ENTRY
11' C.H.

BEDROOM 3
12'-0" X 11'-4"
9' C.H.

UP

PORCH

UP

2-CAR GARAGE
20'-4" X 23'-4"
9' C.H.

BATH

BEDROOM 2
12'-0" X 13'-0"
11' C.H.

70'-8"

50'-4"

© CARMICHAEL & DAME DESIGNS, INC.

$\mathcal{E}$uropean touches and a stucco finish bring a soothing air to this one-story villa. • Identically bayed rooms are steps from the entry, enclosed behind double doors. • An angled kitchen has an efficient layout, and enjoys an open relationship with the breakfast room and family room. • For seclusion, the master suite is separated from two bedrooms.

PLAN 9199-9R
price code 25

CUSTOMIZE
any home plan

Total Living Area   2517 Sq. Ft.

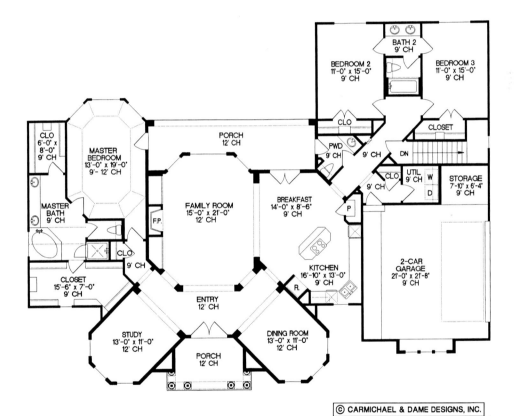

BATH 2
9' CH

BEDROOM 2
11'-0" x 15'-0"
9' CH

BEDROOM 3
11'-0" x 15'-0"
9' CH

CLO

CLOSET

PORCH
12' CH

CLO

PWD
9' CH

9' CH

DN

CLO

UTIL
9' CH

W
D

STORAGE
7'-10" x 6'-4"
9' CH

CLO
6'-0" x
8'-0"
9' CH

MASTER
BEDROOM
13'-0" x 19'-0"
9'- 12' CH

FAMILY ROOM
15'-0" x 21'-0"
12' CH

BREAKFAST
14'-0" x 8'-6"
9' CH

9' CH

MASTER
BATH
9' CH

F.P.

P

2-CAR
GARAGE
21'-0" x 21'-8"
9' CH

CLO

9' CH

KITCHEN
16'-10" x 13'-0"
9' CH

R

CLOSET
15'-6" x 7'-0"
9' CH

ENTRY
12' CH

STUDY
13'-0" x 11'-0"
12' CH

PORCH
12' CH

DINING ROOM
13'-0" x 11'-0"
12' CH

59'-0"

77'-0"

© CARMICHAEL & DAME DESIGNS, INC.

Call toll-free
800-947-7526
www.designbasics.com

27

Stonelake Manor

*M*ultiple hips create contrast, complementing this exterior's stone and stucco finishes. • A corner fireplace offers an accent in the family room, which connects to a rear porch. • All three secondary bedrooms have walk-in closets and private access to a bath. • They are strategically separated from the master suite.

PLAN 9200-9R

price code 26

Call toll-free
800-947-7526
www.designbasics.com

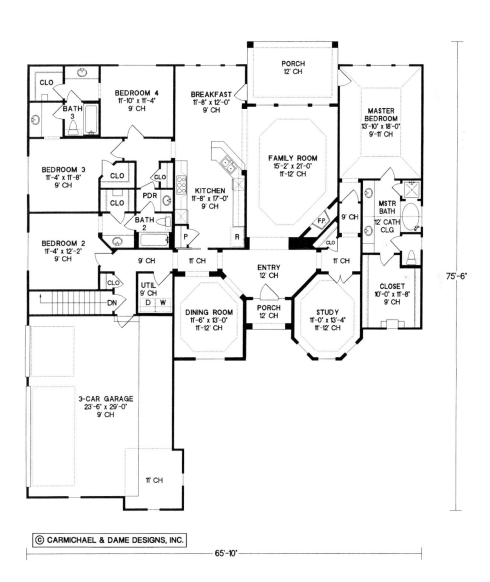

© CARMICHAEL & DAME DESIGNS, INC.

Total Living Area   2679 Sq. Ft.

*I*t's not surprising that the majority of homes in this second collection of designs by Carmichael & Dame are 1 1/2-story designs – two-level homes with the master suite located on the main level. Many people enjoy the way they "live" like a one-story, especially the accessibility of the master suite. But as Dame expressed in the homes on the following pages, positioning additional bedrooms on the upper level leaves space to include studies, main-level guest suites or even extra elaborate master suites. With the master suite on the main level, bonus rooms and game rooms often accompany the additional bedrooms on the upper level. These upper level bedrooms blend with the main floor when paired with the two-story living spaces found in these 1 1/2-story homes. Strategically placed balconies and catwalks connect the second floor bedrooms with the dramatic main level views.

1-1/2 Story Homes

Wilshire Showcase

Palladian windows framing a front porch define the charming nature of this home. • Vaulted ceilings adorn the bedrooms contributing to a feeling of spaciousness. • French doors bring light and connectivity to the breakfast area. • Plenty of storage is provided in the garage, making it ideal for a work and recycling center.

Call toll-free
800-947-7526
www.designbasics.com

PLAN 9209-9R

price code 18

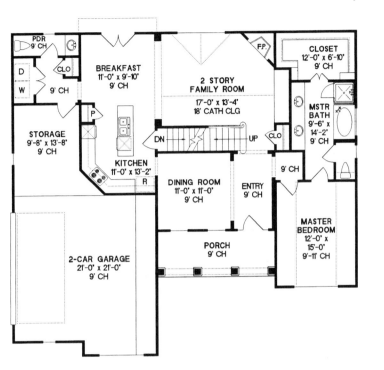

PDR
9' CH

D
W
9' CH

CLO

BREAKFAST
11'-0" x 9'-10"
9' CH

2 STORY
FAMILY ROOM
17'-0" x 13'-4"
18' CATH CLG

FP.

CLOSET
12'-0" x 6'-10"
9' CH

MSTR
BATH
9'-6" x
14'-2"
9' CH

STORAGE
9'-8" x 13'-8"
9' CH

P

KITCHEN
11'-0" x 13'-2"

R

DN   UP

CLO

9' CH

DINING ROOM
11'-0" x 11'-0"
9' CH

ENTRY
9' CH

MASTER
BEDROOM
12'-0" x
15'-0"
9'-11" CH

2-CAR GARAGE
21'-0" x 21'-0"
9' CH

PORCH
9' CH

47'-0"

© CARMICHAEL & DAME DESIGNS, INC.

52'-0"

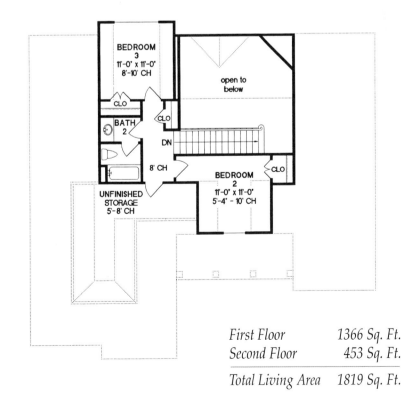

BEDROOM
3
11'-0" x 11'-0"
8'-10' CH

open to
below

CLO

CLO

BATH
2

DN

8' CH

CLO

BEDROOM
2
11'-0" x 11'-0"
5'-4" - 10' CH

UNFINISHED
STORAGE
5'-8' CH

First Floor	*1366 Sq. Ft.*
Second Floor	*453 Sq. Ft.*
Total Living Area	*1819 Sq. Ft.*

Unfinished Storage adds 217 Sq. Ft.

Del Monte Manor

The main living areas of this design are concentrated to the rear, where a family room with a vaulted ceiling features a bank of windows viewing the backyard. • The kitchen has an eating bar that seats the whole family and a nearby veranda provides a place to enjoy the outdoors.

Call toll-free
800-947-7526
www.designbasics.com

PLAN 9175-9R
price code 18

MASTER BATH
9'-11' CH

9' CH

F.P.

MASTER BEDROOM
12'-0' x 15'-0'
9'-11' CH

9' CH

CLO
6'-0' x 10'-0'
9' CH

W. D.

UTIL
9' CH

PWD
9' CH

BRKFST
9'-0' x 9'-0'
9' CH

PORCH
12' CH

UP

DN.

CLO

PAN

FAMILY ROOM
17'-6' x 14'-0'
12'-16' CH

2-CAR GARAGE
25'-8' x 26'-0'
9' CH

KITCHEN
11'-0' x 13'-0'
9' CH

R.

52'-10'

F.P.

DINING ROOM
11'-0' x 12'-0'
9' CH

ENTRY
12' CH

PORCH
12' CH

CLO.

52'-11'

© CARMICHAEL & DAME DESIGNS, INC.

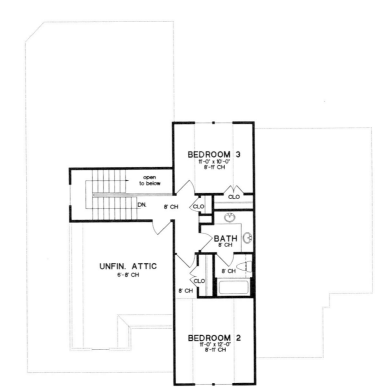

BEDROOM 3
11'-0' x 10'-0'
8'-11' CH

open to below

DN.

8' CH

CLO

CLO

BATH
8' CH

8' CH

UNFIN. ATTIC
6'-8' CH

CLO

8' CH

BEDROOM 2
11'-0' x 12'-0'
8'-11' CH

First Floor   1387 Sq. Ft.
Second Floor   471 Sq. Ft.

Total Living Area   1858 Sq. Ft.

Unfinished Attic adds 243 Sq. Ft.

Sherwood Estate

*S*quare windows bring additional light into the study and an upper-level bedroom in this design. • An angled fireplace can be viewed from both the kitchen and dining area, which share an open arrangement with the family room. • A large window in the master suite frames a rear view, while French doors lead to a restful bath.

Call toll-free
800-947-7526
www.designbasics.com

PLAN 9195-9R

price code 19

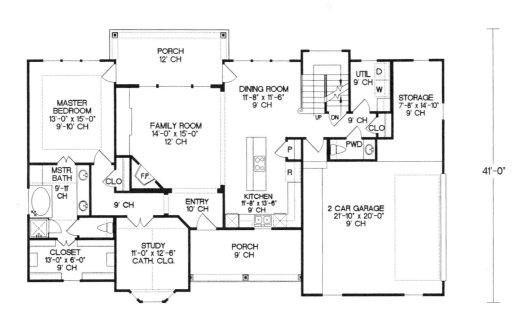

PORCH
12' CH

MASTER BEDROOM
13'-0" x 15'-0"
9'-10' CH

FAMILY ROOM
14'-0" x 15'-0"
12' CH

DINING ROOM
11'-8" x 11'-6"
9' CH

UTIL
9' CH

D / W

STORAGE
7'-8" x 14'-10"
9' CH

MSTR. BATH
9'-11'
CH

CLO

F.P.

9' CH

CLO

P

R

PWD

KITCHEN
11'-8" x 13'-6"
9' CH

ENTRY
10' CH

CLOSET
13'-0" x 6'-0"
9' CH

STUDY
11'-0" x 12'-6"
CATH. CLG.

PORCH
9' CH

2 CAR GARAGE
21'-10" x 20'-0"
9' CH

41'-0"

© CARMICHAEL & DAME DESIGNS, INC.

64'-4"

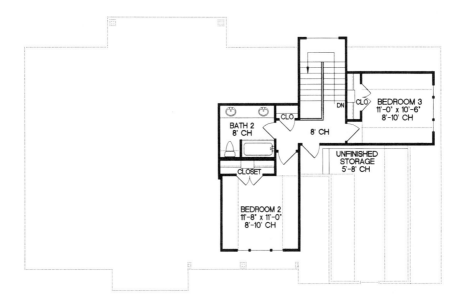

BATH 2
8' CH

CLO

8' CH

DN

CLO

BEDROOM 3
11'-0" x 10'-6"
8'-10' CH

UNFINISHED STORAGE
5'-8' CH

CLOSET

BEDROOM 2
11'-8" x 11'-0"
8'-10' CH

ORIGINAL DRAFT
ALL PLANS HAVE BEEN REGISTERED
WITH THE U.S. COPYRIGHT OFFICE

First Floor	1446 Sq. Ft.
Second Floor	456 Sq. Ft.
Total Living Area	1902 Sq. Ft.

Unfinished Storage adds 282 Sq. Ft.

Buckland Showcase

*T*his design seems to have something for everyone. • The kitchen, breakfast and living rooms share communal space for family time together. • A formal dining room provides a place to entertain. • An upper-level hallway provides drama, showcasing a balcony that overlooks the two-story living room.

Call toll-free
800-947-7526
www.designbasics.com

PLAN 9170-9R

price code 19

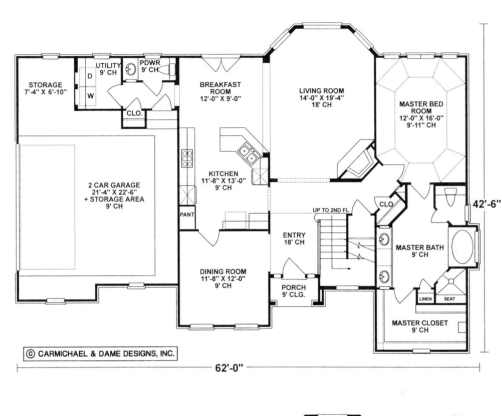

STORAGE
7'-4" X 6'-10"

UTILITY
9' CH

PDWR
9' CH

CLO.

BREAKFAST
ROOM
12'-0" X 9'-0"

LIVING ROOM
14'-0" X 19'-4"
18' CH

MASTER BED
ROOM
12'-0" X 16'-0"
9'-11" CH

2 CAR GARAGE
21'-4" X 22'-6"
+ STORAGE AREA
9' CH

KITCHEN
11'-8" X 13'-0"
9' CH

PANT

ENTRY
18' CH

UP TO 2ND FL

CLO

MASTER BATH
9' CH

42'-6"

DINING ROOM
11'-8" X 12'-0"
9' CH

PORCH
9' CLG.

LINEN   SEAT

MASTER CLOSET
9' CH

© CARMICHAEL & DAME DESIGNS, INC.

62'-0"

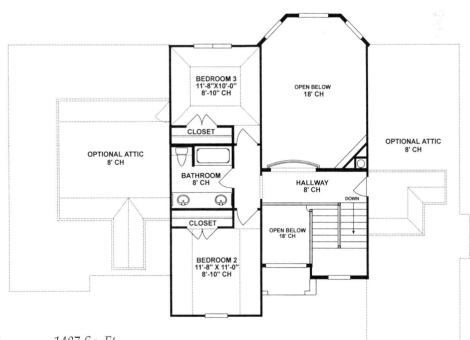

BEDROOM 3
11'-8"X10'-0"
8'-10" CH

OPEN BELOW
18' CH

OPTIONAL ATTIC
8' CH

CLOSET

OPTIONAL ATTIC
8' CH

BATHROOM
8' CH

HALLWAY
8' CH

DOWN

CLOSET

OPEN BELOW
18' CH

BEDROOM 2
11'-8" X 11'-0"
8'-10" CH

First Floor	1487 Sq. Ft.
Second Floor	497 Sq. Ft.
Total Living Area	1984 Sq. Ft.

Unfinished Attic Space adds 329 Sq. Ft.

Deerwood Manor

The family room is central in this traditionally-styled home and is visible from an upper-level balcony. • Bayed windows bring light into the dining room. • An open kitchen interacts with the breakfast and family rooms via its large island with snack bar and its nearby pantry. • Unfinished storage areas inspire places for play or study on the upper level.

Call toll-free
800-947-7526
www.designbasics.com

40

PLAN 9208-9R

price code 21

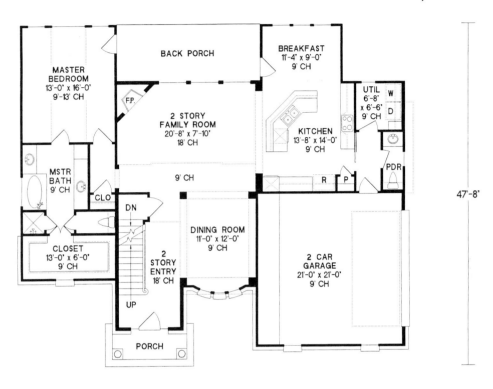

BACK PORCH

BREAKFAST
11'-4" x 9'-0"
9' CH

MASTER
BEDROOM
13'-0" x 16'-0"
9'-13' CH

F.P.

2 STORY
FAMILY ROOM
20'-8" x 7'-10"
18' CH

KITCHEN
13'-8" x 14'-0"
9' CH

UTIL
6'-8"
x 6'-6"
9' CH

W
D

9' CH

MSTR
BATH
9' CH

PDR

CLO

9' CH

R   P

DN

CLOSET
13'-0" x 6'-0"
9' CH

2
STORY
ENTRY
18' CH

DINING ROOM
11'-0" x 12'-0"
9' CH

2 CAR
GARAGE
21'-0" x 21'-0"
9' CH

UP

47'-8"

PORCH

© CARMICHAEL & DAME DESIGNS, INC.

57'-1 1/2"

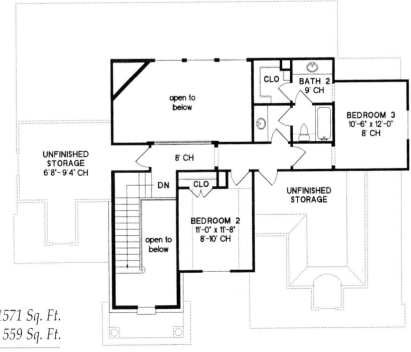

CLO

BATH 2
9' CH

open to
below

BEDROOM 3
10'-6" x 12'-0"
8' CH

UNFINISHED
STORAGE
6'8"-9'4" CH

8' CH

DN

CLO

UNFINISHED
STORAGE

BEDROOM 2
11'-0" x 11'-8"
8'-10' CH

open to
below

First Floor   1571 Sq. Ft.
Second Floor   559 Sq. Ft.
─────────────────────────────────
Total Living Area   2130 Sq. Ft.

Unfinished Storage adds 249 Sq. Ft.

Memorial Manor

A stair tower generates interest both inside and on the exterior of this home. • A wrap-around porch hugs a sun room/dining room, beckoning relaxation. Ideal for casual living, the family room shares space with a breakfast bay topped by a vaulted ceiling.

Call toll-free
800-947-7526
www.designbasics.com

PLAN 9188-9R
price code 21

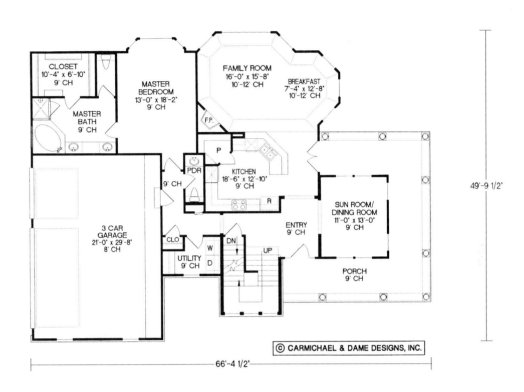

CLOSET
10'-4" x 6'-10"
9' CH

MASTER
BEDROOM
13'-0" x 18'-2"
9' CH

FAMILY ROOM
16'-0" x 15'-8"
10'-12' CH

BREAKFAST
7'-4" x 12'-8"
10'-12' CH

MASTER
BATH
9' CH

F.P.

PDR

P

KITCHEN
18'-6" x 12'-10"
9' CH

R

9' CH

3 CAR
GARAGE
21'-0" x 29'-8"
8' CH

CLO

SUN ROOM/
DINING ROOM
11'-0" x 13'-0"
9' CH

ENTRY
9' CH

W

D

DN

UP

UTILITY
9' CH

PORCH
9' CH

49'-9 1/2'

© CARMICHAEL & DAME DESIGNS, INC.

66'-4 1/2'

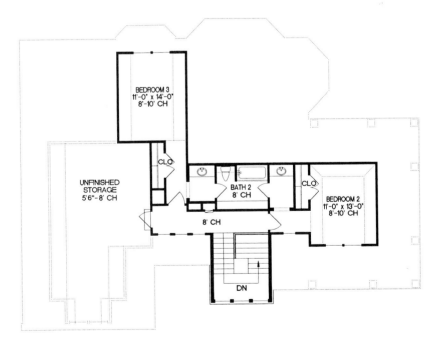

BEDROOM 3
11'-0" x 14'-0"
8'-10' CH

UNFINISHED
STORAGE
5'6"-8' CH

CLO

BATH 2
8' CH

CLO

BEDROOM 2
11'-0" x 13'-0"
8'-10' CH

8' CH

DN

First Floor   1531 Sq. Ft.
Second Floor   657 Sq. Ft.

Total Living Area   2188 Sq. Ft.

Unfinished Storage adds 425 Sq. Ft.

Oak Crest Manor

*A*n elevated study helps give the windows on the facade a symmetrical balance. • Located midway up a U-shaped staircase, the study is entered through an arched opening. • A corner fireplace is paired with built-in entertainment shelves in the living room, which also features views from an upper-level balcony and through the bayed windows in back.

PLAN 9180-9R

price code 22

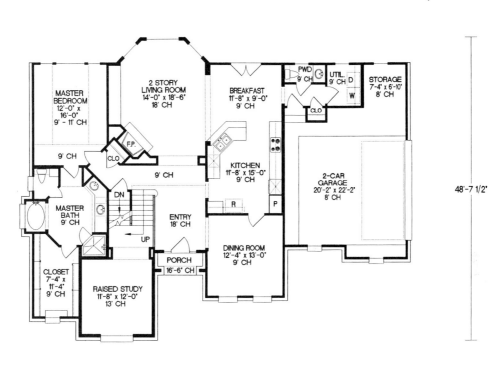

MASTER
BEDROOM
12'-0" x
16'-0"
9' - 11' CH

2 STORY
LIVING ROOM
14'-0" x 18'-6"
18' CH

BREAKFAST
11'-8" x 9'-0"
9' CH

PWD
9' CH

UTIL.
9' CH

STORAGE
7'-4" x 6'-10"
8' CH

D
W

9' CH

CLO

F.P.

CLO

9' CH

KITCHEN
11'-8" x 15'-0"
9' CH

2-CAR
GARAGE
20'-2" x 22'-2"
8' CH

MASTER
BATH
9' CH

DN

UP

ENTRY
18' CH

R

P

CLOSET
7'-4" x
11'-4"
9' CH

RAISED STUDY
11'-8" x 12'-0"
13' CH

PORCH
16'-6" CH

DINING ROOM
12'-4" x 13'-0"
9' CH

48'-7 1/2"

© CARMICHAEL & DAME DESIGNS, INC.

63'-3"

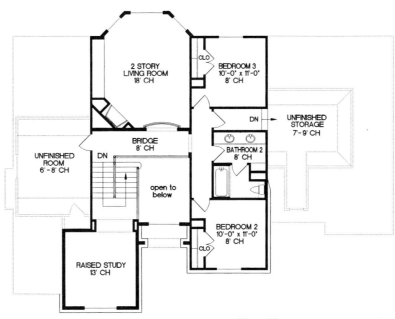

2 STORY
LIVING ROOM
18' CH

CLO

BEDROOM 3
10'-0" x 11'-0"
8' CH

DN

UNFINISHED
STORAGE
7-9' CH

BRIDGE
8' CH

BATHROOM 2
8' CH

UNFINISHED
ROOM
6'-8' CH

DN

open to
below

RAISED STUDY
13' CH

BEDROOM 2
10'-0" x 11'-0"
8' CH

CLO

Call toll-free
800-947-7526
www.designbasics.com

First Floor	1776 Sq. Ft.
Second Floor	461 Sq. Ft.
Total Living Area	2237 Sq. Ft.

Unfinished Areas add 354 Sq. Ft.

45

Wortham Manor

*R*epetitive gables meet a copper-clad roof above this home's front porch. • Double-hung windows increase the home's old-fashioned appeal. • A covered veranda wraps around the rear of the home and is enjoyed visually from the U-shaped staircase, two-story family room and breakfast room.

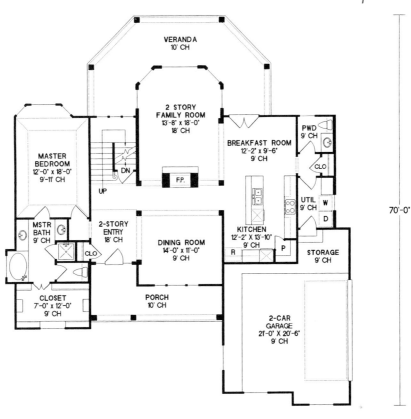

VERANDA
10' CH

2 STORY
FAMILY ROOM
13'-8" x 18'-0"
18' CH

BREAKFAST ROOM
12'-2" x 9'-6"
9' CH

PWD
9' CH

CLO

MASTER
BEDROOM
12'-0" x 18'-0"
9'-11" CH

DN

UP

F.P.

UTIL
9' CH

W

D

MSTR
BATH
9' CH

2-STORY
ENTRY
18' CH

KITCHEN
12'-2" X 13'-10"
9' CH

R

P

CLO

DINING ROOM
14'-0" x 11'-0"
9' CH

STORAGE
9' CH

CLOSET
7'-0" x 12'-0"
9' CH

PORCH
10' CH

2-CAR
GARAGE
21'-0" X 20'-6"
9' CH

70'-0"

57'-8"

© CARMICHAEL & DAME DESIGNS, INC.

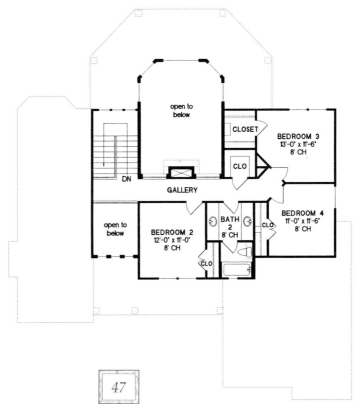

open to
below

CLOSET

BEDROOM 3
13'-0" x 11'-6"
8' CH

CLO

DN

GALLERY

CLO

BATH
2
8' CH

CLO

open to
below

BEDROOM 2
12'-0" x 11'-0"
8' CH

BEDROOM 4
11'-0" x 11'-6"
8' CH

CLO

First Floor	1568 Sq. Ft.
Second Floor	733 Sq. Ft.
Total Living Area	2301 Sq. Ft.

Call toll-free
800-947-7526
www.designbasics.com

Troon Manor

$\mathcal{S}$hared space is important in this design, especially in its large living room, which is open to the kitchen and breakfast room. Three sets of French doors open onto a rear sun deck. • The living room can also be enjoyed from a second-level balcony and study loft.

Call toll-free
800-947-7526
www.designbasics.com

48

PLAN 9166-9R
price code 23

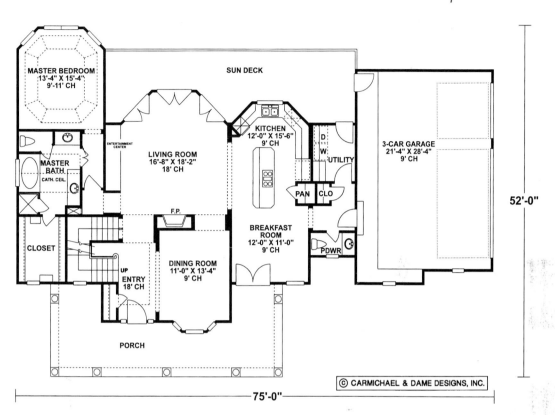

MASTER BEDROOM
13'-4" X 15'-4"
9'-11' CH

SUN DECK

KITCHEN
12'-0" X 15'-6"
9' CH

3-CAR GARAGE
21'-4" X 28'-4"
9' CH

ENTERTAINMENT CENTER

LIVING ROOM
16'-8" X 18'-2"
18' CH

D
W

UTILITY

MASTER BATH
CATH. CEIL.

PAN

CLO

F.P.

BREAKFAST ROOM
12'-0" X 11'-0"
9' CH

CLOSET

DINING ROOM
11'-0" X 13'-4"
9' CH

PDWR

UP

ENTRY
18' CH

PORCH

52'-0"

75'-0"

© CARMICHAEL & DAME DESIGNS, INC.

STUDY LOFT
8'-0" X 12'-0"
8' CH

LIVING ROOM BELOW
18' CH

BEDROOM 2
12'-4" X 13'-4"
8' CH

BALCONY

DN

CATH. CEIL.

W.I.C.

BATH

BEDROOM 3
12'-2" x 13'-0"
8' CH

18' CLG.

LEDGE

First Floor	1649 Sq. Ft.
Second Floor	712 Sq. Ft.
Total Living Area	2361 Sq. Ft.

49

South Hampton

A long view extends from the open study through the stair hall and into the dining room with bayed window. • An unfinished storage area rests on the second level, along with two bedrooms that each have their own vanities. • A family room fireplace creates a warming view from the breakfast area.

Call toll-free
800-947-7526
www.designbasics.com

PLAN 9190-9R

price code 23

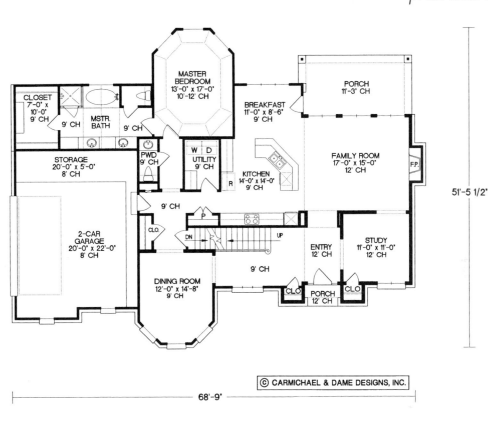

CLOSET
7'-0" x
10'-0"
9' CH

MSTR.
BATH
9' CH

MASTER
BEDROOM
13'-0" x 17'-0"
10'-12' CH

9' CH

BREAKFAST
11'-0" x 8'-6"
9' CH

PORCH
11'-3" CH

STORAGE
20'-0" x 5'-0"
8' CH

PWD
9' CH

W D
UTILITY
9' CH

KITCHEN
14'-0" x 14'-0"
9' CH

R

FAMILY ROOM
17'-0" x 15'-0"
12' CH

F.P.

9' CH

CLO.

P

UP

DN

STUDY
11'-0" x 11'-0"
12' CH

2-CAR
GARAGE
20'-0" x 22'-0"
8' CH

DINING ROOM
12'-0" x 14'-8"
9' CH

9' CH

ENTRY
12' CH

CLO

PORCH
12' CH

CLO

51'-5 1/2'

68'-9"

© CARMICHAEL & DAME DESIGNS, INC.

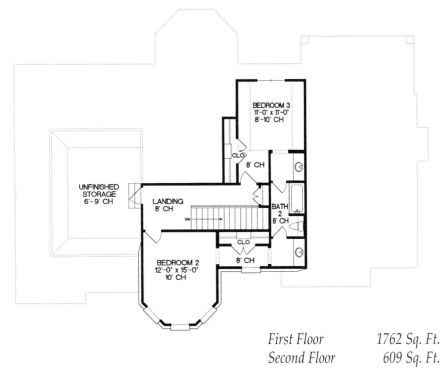

UNFINISHED
STORAGE
6'-9" CH

LANDING
8' CH

DN

BEDROOM 3
11'-0" x 11'-0"
8'-10' CH

CLO
8' CH

BATH
2
8' CH

CLO
8' CH

BEDROOM 2
12'-0" x 15'-0"
10' CH

First Floor	1762 Sq. Ft.
Second Floor	609 Sq. Ft.
Total Living Area	2371 Sq. Ft.

Unfinished Storage adds 310 Sq. Ft.

Heritage Manor

$\mathcal{S}$tone dominates the front of this attractive home, granting it the feel of an English country estate. • An amazing window overtakes the front of the study with a ceiling more than 13 feet high. • The kitchen comfortably serves the family room with a peninsula island with snack bar. • A circular staircase adds airiness to the home and leads to three upper-level bedrooms.

Call toll-free
800-947-7526
www.designbasics.com

52

PLAN 9203-9R
price code 25

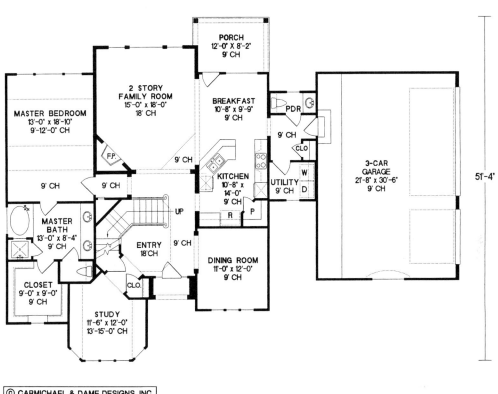

PORCH
12'-0" X 8'-2"
9' CH

2 STORY
FAMILY ROOM
15'-0" x 18'-0"
18' CH

BREAKFAST
10'-8" x 9'-9"
9' CH

PDR

MASTER BEDROOM
13'-0" x 18'-10"
9'-12'-0" CH

9' CH

CLO

3-CAR
GARAGE
21'-8" x 30'-6"
9' CH

F.P.

9' CH

9' CH

9' CH

KITCHEN
10'-8" x
14'-0"
9' CH

UTILITY
9' CH

W
D

51'-4'

MASTER
BATH
13'-0" x 8'-4"
9' CH

UP

R

P

ENTRY
18'CH

9' CH

DINING ROOM
11'-0" x 12'-0"
9' CH

CLOSET
9'-0" x 9'-0"
9' CH

CLO.

STUDY
11'-6' x 12'-0"
13'-15'-0" CH

© CARMICHAEL & DAME DESIGNS, INC.

70'-2"

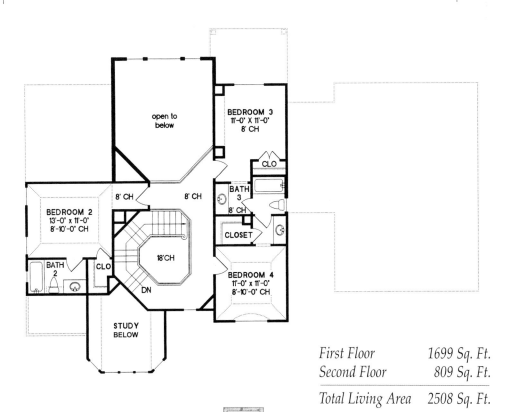

open to
below

BEDROOM 3
11'-0" X 11'-0"
8' CH

CLO

BEDROOM 2
13'-0" x 11'-0"
8'-10'-0" CH

8' CH

8' CH

BATH
3
8' CH

CLOSET

BATH
2

CLO

18'CH

DN

BEDROOM 4
11'-0" x 11'-0"
8'-10'-0" CH

STUDY
BELOW

First Floor	1699 *Sq. Ft.*
Second Floor	809 *Sq. Ft.*
Total Living Area	2508 *Sq. Ft.*

Chasleton Manor

A connected sun room and family room are central to this home. • A beamed cathedral ceiling is visible from the stairwell and an upper-level balcony. • Traffic circulates around a see-through fireplace. • Connection to a front wrap-around veranda is a natural extension of the living space.

Call toll-free
800-947-7526
www.designbasics.com

MASTER
BEDROOM
13'-0" x 18'-0"
9'-12' CH

FP

MASTER
BATH
9' CH

BACK PORCH
9' CH

BREAKFAST
9'-0" x 11'-4"
9' CH

KITCHEN
9' CH

MASTER
CLOSET
9' CH

55'-11 1/2"

SUN ROOM
11'-4" x 15'-0"
CATHEDRAL CLG.
12' to 19' CH

FAMILY ROOM
15'-9" x 15'-0"
12' to 19' CH

FP

PWDR
9' CH

UTILITY
9' CH

W
D

DOWN TO
BSMT

PAN

ENTRY
UP

DINING ROOM
11'-4" x 13'-0"
9' CH

2-CAR GARAGE
21'-8" x 24'-10"
10'-4" CH

VERANDA
9' CH

STORAGE

© CARMICHAEL & DAME DESIGNS, INC.

66'-0"

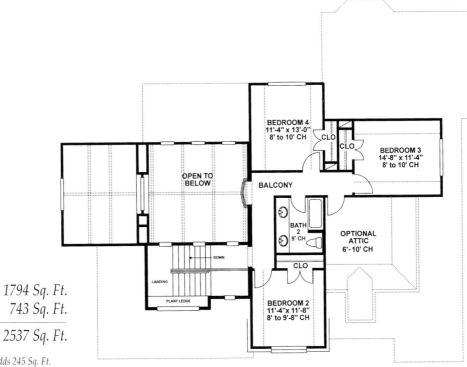

BEDROOM 4
11'-4" x 13'-0"
8' to 10' CH

CLO

CLO

BEDROOM 3
14'-8" x 11'-4"
8' to 10' CH

OPEN TO
BELOW

BALCONY

BATH
2
9' CH

OPTIONAL
ATTIC
6'-10' CH

CLO

DOWN

LANDING

PLANT LEDGE

BEDROOM 2
11'-4" x 11'-8"
8' to 9'-8" CH

First Floor	1794 Sq. Ft.
Second Floor	743 Sq. Ft.
Total Living Area	2537 Sq. Ft.

Unfinished Attic Space adds 245 Sq. Ft.

Sheidan Manor

A porte cochere offers versatility to this design, especially if built with a detached garage. • A wrap-around veranda leads inside where an eight-sided family room offers angles of glass and a hearth. • Adjacent to a dual-sink vanity and walk-in closet in the master bath is the privacy of a whirlpool tub.

Call toll-free
800-947-7526
www.designbasics.com

56

PLAN 9205-9R
price code 25

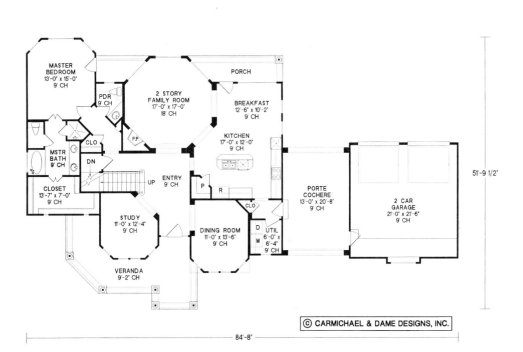

MASTER BEDROOM
13'-0" x 15'-0"
9' CH

PDR
9' CH

2 STORY FAMILY ROOM
17'-0" x 17'-0"
18' CH

PORCH

BREAKFAST
12'-6" x 10'-2"
9' CH

CLO

FP

KITCHEN
17'-0" x 12'-0"
9' CH

MSTR BATH
9' CH

DN

ENTRY
9' CH

P

R

PORTE COCHERE
13'-0" x 20'-8"
9' CH

2 CAR GARAGE
21'-0" x 21'-6"
9' CH

CLOSET
13'-7" x 7'-0"
9' CH

UP

CLO

STUDY
11'-0" x 12'-4"
9' CH

DINING ROOM
11'-0" x 13'-6"
9' CH

D
W

UTIL
6'-0" x 6'-4"
9' CH

VERANDA
9'-2" CH

51'-9 1/2"

84'-8"

© CARMICHAEL & DAME DESIGNS, INC.

open to below

BEDROOM 2
13'-2" x 12'-0"
8'-10' CH

8' CH

DN

BATH 2

BATH 3

CLO

8' CH

CLO

BEDROOM 3
11'-0" x 12'-4"
8' CH

CLO

BEDROOM 4
11'-0" x 12'-0"
8'-10' CH

First Floor   1729 Sq. Ft.
Second Floor   847 Sq. Ft.

Total Living Area   2576 Sq. Ft.

ALL PLANS HAVE BEEN REGISTERED · ORIGINAL DRAFT · WITH THE U.S. COPYRIGHT OFFICE

Briar Chase

A series of arched and porthole windows provide interesting repetition on this home's exterior. • Large main-level living spaces seem meant for entertaining. • The two-story family and living rooms enjoy staircases that merge and openly climb to the second level.

Call toll-free
800-947-7526
www.designbasics.com

PLAN 9178-9R

price code 25

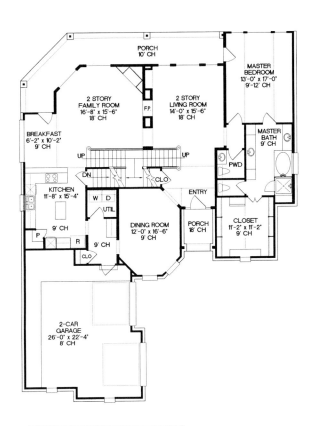

PORCH
10' CH

MASTER
BEDROOM
13'-0" x 17'-0"
9'-12' CH

2 STORY
FAMILY ROOM
16'-8" x 15'-6"
18' CH

2 STORY
LIVING ROOM
14'-0" x 15'-6"
18' CH

F.P.

BREAKFAST
6'-2" x 10'-2"
9' CH

MASTER
BATH
9' CH

UP   UP

DN

KITCHEN
11'-8" x 15'-4"

PWD

CLO

ENTRY

W   D

UTIL

9' CH

DINING ROOM
12'-0" x 16'-6"
9' CH

PORCH
18' CH

CLOSET
11'-2" x 11'-2"
9' CH

P

R

9' CH

CLO

2-CAR
GARAGE
26'-0" x 22'-4"
8' CH

70'-0"

© CARMICHAEL & DAME DESIGNS, INC.

54'-0"

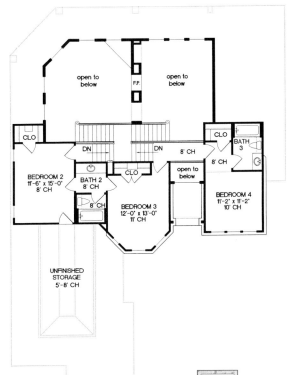

open to
below

open to
below

F.P.

CLO

CLO

BATH
3

DN   DN   8' CH

8' CH

BEDROOM 2
11'-6" x 15'-0"
8' CH

BATH 2
8' CH

CLO

open to
below

8' CH

BEDROOM 4
11'-2" x 11'-2"
10' CH

BEDROOM 3
12'-0" x 13'-0"
11' CH

UNFINISHED
STORAGE
5'-8' CH

CUSTOMIZE
any home plan

First Floor	1902 Sq. Ft.
Second Floor	686 Sq. Ft.
Total Living Area	2588 Sq. Ft.

Unfinished Storage adds 217 Sq. Ft.

Stanton Showcase

The main living areas of this design are concentrated to the rear, where a two-story family room features a bank of windows viewing the backyard. • The kitchen has an eating bar to seat the whole family and a veranda provides a place to enjoy the outdoors.

Call toll-free
800-947-7526
www.designbasics.com

PLAN 9174-9R

price code 26

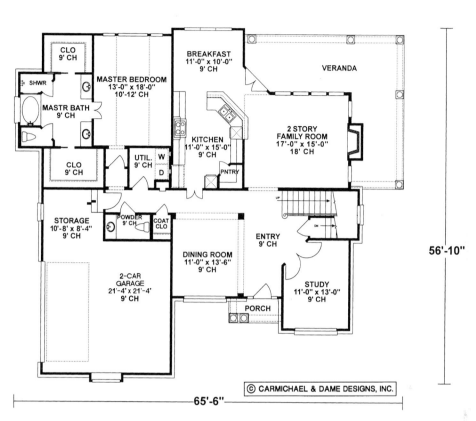

CLO
9' CH

MASTER BEDROOM
13'-0" x 18'-0"
10'-12' CH

BREAKFAST
11'-0" x 10'-0"
9' CH

VERANDA

SHWR

MASTR BATH
9' CH

KITCHEN
11'-0" x 15'-0"
9' CH

2 STORY
FAMILY ROOM
17'-0" x 15'-0"
18' CH

CLO
9' CH

UTIL.
9' CH

W
D

PNTRY

STORAGE
10'-8" x 8'-4"
9' CH

POWDER
9' CH

COAT
CLO

UP

DN

2-CAR
GARAGE
21'-4" x 21'-4"
9' CH

DINING ROOM
11'-0" x 13'-6"
9' CH

ENTRY
9' CH

STUDY
11'-0" x 13'-0"
9' CH

PORCH

56'-10"

© CARMICHAEL & DAME DESIGNS, INC.

65'-6"

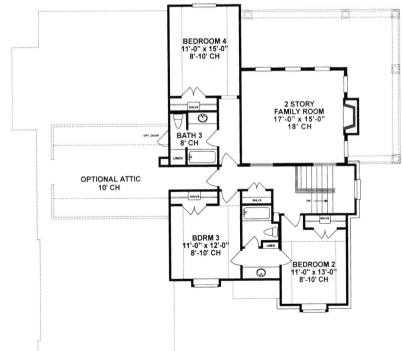

BEDROOM 4
11'-0" x 15'-0"
8'-10' CH

2 STORY
FAMILY ROOM
17'-0" x 15'-0"
18' CH

SHLVS

BATH 3
8' CH

OPT. DOOR

LINEN

OPTIONAL ATTIC
10' CH

SHLVS

DN

SHLVS

BDRM 3
11'-0" x 12'-0"
8'-10' CH

SHLVS

LINEN

BEDROOM 2
11'-0" x 13'-0"
8'-10' CH

First Floor   1844 SQ. FT.
Second Floor   794 SQ. FT.

Total Living Area   2638 SQ. FT.

Unfinished Attic Space adds 324 Sq. Ft.

Wilks Manor

*T*his elevation offers a variety of details to enjoy – a tall chimney, bayed wrought-iron widow's balcony and triple windows set under a hip roof. • Windows on two walls bring light into a winding stair-case that leads to the second level. • Private guest quarters are also located on the main level.

Call toll-free
800-947-7526
www.designbasics.com

PLAN 9165-9R

price code 26

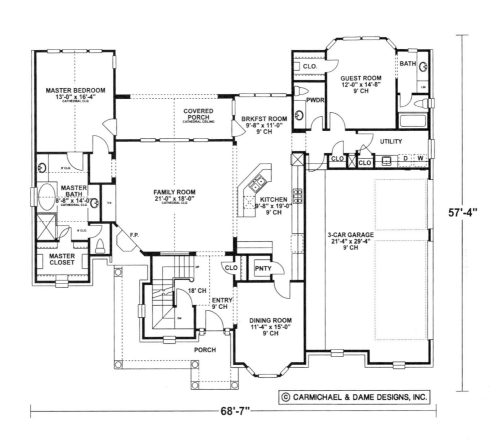

MASTER BEDROOM
13'-0" x 16'-4"
CATHEDRAL CLG

COVERED
PORCH
CATHEDRAL CEILING

BRKFST ROOM
9'-8" x 11'-0"
9' CH

CLO.

PWDR

GUEST ROOM
12'-0" x 14'-8"
9' CH

BATH

LIN

UTILITY

MASTER
BATH
8'-8" x 14'-0"
CATHEDRAL CLG

FAMILY ROOM
21'-0" x 18'-0"
CATHEDRAL CLG

KITCHEN
9'-8" x 19'-0"
9' CH

CLO   CLO   D   W

T.V.

MASTER
CLOSET

F.P.

3-CAR GARAGE
21'-4" x 29'-4"
9' CH

57'-4"

UP

18' CH

CLO   PNTY

ENTRY
9' CH

DM

PORCH

DINING ROOM
11'-4" x 15'-0"
9' CH

© CARMICHAEL & DAME DESIGNS, INC.

68'-7"

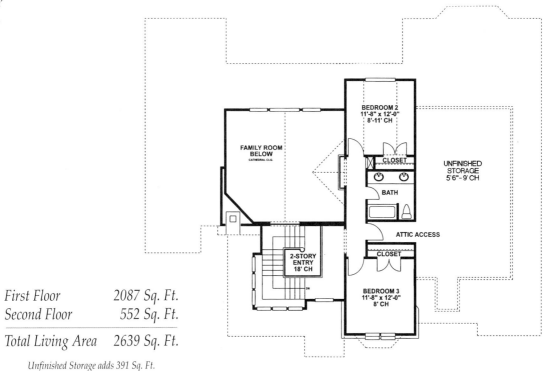

FAMILY ROOM
BELOW
CATHEDRAL CLG.

BEDROOM 2
11'-8" x 12'-0"
8'-11' CH

CLOSET

UNFINISHED
STORAGE
5'6"- 9' CH

BATH

ATTIC ACCESS

2-STORY
ENTRY
18' CH

CLOSET

BEDROOM 3
11'-8" x 12'-0"
8' CH

DM

First Floor   2087 Sq. Ft.
Second Floor   552 Sq. Ft.

Total Living Area   2639 Sq. Ft.

Unfinished Storage adds 391 Sq. Ft.

The open room arrangement in this design allows the study, dining room, kitchen and breakfast room to be viewed from the family room. • The master suite enjoys its access to the rear porch as much as its accompanying bath with twin vanities and whirlpool tub.

Call toll-free
800-947-7526
www.designbasics.com

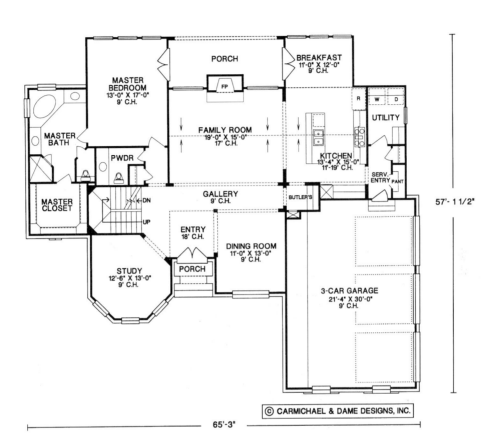

PORCH

BREAKFAST
11'-0" X 12'-0"
9' C.H.

MASTER BEDROOM
13'-0" X 17'-0"
9' C.H.

FP

UTILITY

R   W   D

MASTER BATH

FAMILY ROOM
19'-0" X 15'-0"
17' C.H.

PWDR

KITCHEN
13'-4" X 15'-0"
11'-19' C.H.

MASTER CLOSET

DN

UP

GALLERY
9' C.H.

SERV. ENTRY PANT

BUTLER'S

ENTRY
18' C.H.

DINING ROOM
11'-0" X 13'-0"
9' C.H.

57'- 1 1/2"

STUDY
12'-6" X 13'-0"
9' C.H.

PORCH

3-CAR GARAGE
21'-4" X 30'-0"
9' C.H.

© CARMICHAEL & DAME DESIGNS, INC.

65'-3"

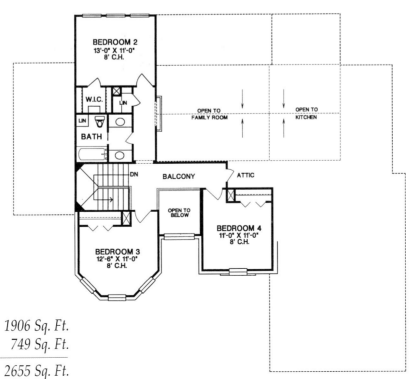

BEDROOM 2
13'-0" X 11'-0"
8' C.H.

W.I.C.   LIN

LIN

BATH

OPEN TO FAMILY ROOM

OPEN TO KITCHEN

DN

BALCONY   **ATTIC**

OPEN TO BELOW

BEDROOM 4
11'-0" X 11'-0"
8' C.H.

BEDROOM 3
12'-6" X 11'-0"
8' C.H.

First Floor	*1906 Sq. Ft.*
Second Floor	*749 Sq. Ft.*
Total Living Area	*2655 Sq. Ft.*

A main-level study is secluded at the front of this design with a full bath nearby, making it an ideal choice to use as an additional bedroom. • The back porch is joined by the breakfast room and master suite and is ideal for entertaining. • Near the upper level bedrooms, a large playroom has built-in shelves.

Call toll-free
800-947-7526
www.designbasics.com

BACK PORCH
12' CH

CLO.
6'-8" x
12'-8"
9' CH

MSTR. BEDROOM
13'-0" x 16'-0"
9'-10" CH

BRKFST.
11'-4" x 11'-7 1/2"
9' CH

T V

FAMILY ROOM
15'-0" x 20'-0"
12' CH

F.P.

MSTR.
BATH
9' CH

UTIL.
9' CH
D W

CLO.

KITCHEN
11'-10" X 16'-0"
9' CH

UP

DN

PAN.

R

3-CAR
GARAGE
23'-10" X 32'-0"
9' CH

GALLERY
9' CH

DINING ROOM
14'-8" x 11'-4"
9' CH

ENTRY
9' CH

CLO

BATH
9' CH

CLO.

STUDY/BEDROOM 2
12'-0" x 11'-0"
9' CH

70'-4 1/2"

© CARMICHAEL & DAME DESIGNS, INC.

50'-7"

CUSTOMIZE
any home plan

UNFINISHED
STORAGE
6'-8" CH

CLO.
8' CH

PLAY ROOM
8' CH

CLO.

DN

BEDROOM 3
12'-0" X 12'-0"
8' CH

BATH
8' CH

CLO.

BEDROOM 4
12'-0" X 11'-7"
8' CH

First Floor	1924 Sq. Ft.
Second Floor	741 Sq. Ft.
Total Living Area	2665 Sq. Ft.

Unfinished Storage adds 548 Sq. Ft.

Eaglewood Manor

A pair of towers extend skyward on this home's elevation, showcasing an array of beautiful windows. • A wide entry grants access to the study or dining room – both of which view the front. • Ideally secluded behind a three-car garage, the master bedroom features a vaulted ceiling and corner whirlpool tub.

Call toll-free
800-947-7526
www.designbasics.com

PLAN 9196-9R
price code 27

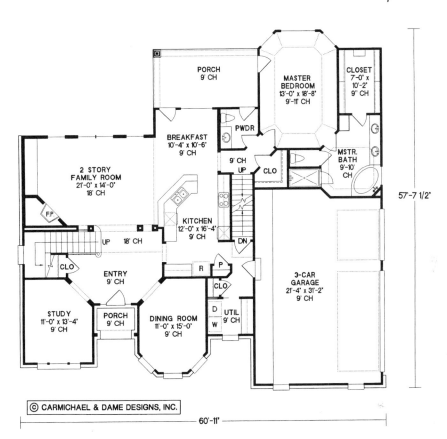

PORCH
9' CH

MASTER BEDROOM
13'-0" x 18'-8"
9'-11' CH

CLOSET
7'-0" x
10'-2"
9" CH

BREAKFAST
10'-4" x 10'-6"
9' CH

PWDR

9' CH
UP

CLO

MSTR. BATH
9'-10'
CH

2 STORY FAMILY ROOM
21'-0" x 14'-0"
18' CH

KITCHEN
12'-0" x 16'-4"
9' CH

F.P.

UP   18' CH

DN

57'-7 1/2'

CLO

ENTRY
9' CH

R   P

CLO

3-CAR GARAGE
21'-4" x 31'-2"
9' CH

STUDY
11'-0" x 13'-4"
9' CH

PORCH
9' CH

DINING ROOM
11'-0" x 15'-0"
9' CH

D   **UTIL**
W   9' CH

© CARMICHAEL & DAME DESIGNS, INC.

60'-11"

open to below

BEDROOM 4
11'-0" x 11'-0"
8'-11' CH

CLOSET

8' CH

BATH 3
8' CH

UNFINISHED STORAGE
5'-9'CH

18' CH

DN   8' CH

DN

CLOSET

CLOSET

BEDROOM 3
11'-0" x 11'-0"
8'-11' CH

BATH 2
8' CH

BEDROOM 2
11'-0" x 12'-8"
11' CH

First Floor   1908 Sq. Ft.
Second Floor   869 Sq. Ft.

Total Living Area   2777 Sq. Ft.

Unfinished Storage adds 506 Sq. Ft.

Timber Crest

An arched opening introduces the kitchen with walk-in pantry, large eating bar and island with cooktop. • French doors connect a dining room with columns and a view to the front. • The three dormers on the exterior of this home are enjoyed by two upper-level bedrooms and a bath.

Call toll-free
800-947-7526
www.designbasics.com

PLAN 9179-9R
price code 28

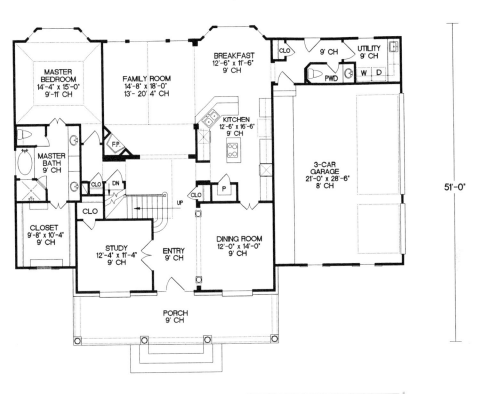

MASTER
BEDROOM
14'-4" x 15'-0"
9'-11' CH

FAMILY ROOM
14'-8" x 18'-0"
13'- 20' 4" CH

BREAKFAST
12'-6" x 11'-6"
9' CH

CLO

9' CH

UTILITY
9' CH

W D

PWD

MASTER
BATH
9' CH

F.P.

KITCHEN
12'-6" x 16'-6"
9' CH

3-CAR
GARAGE
21'-0" x 28'-6"
8' CH

51'-0"

CLO

DN

CLO

CLO

P

CLOSET
9'-8" x 10'-4"
9' CH

CLO

UP

STUDY
12'-4" x 11'-4"
9' CH

ENTRY
9' CH

DINING ROOM
12'-0" x 14'-0"
9' CH

PORCH
9' CH

© CARMICHAEL & DAME DESIGNS, INC.

64'-8"

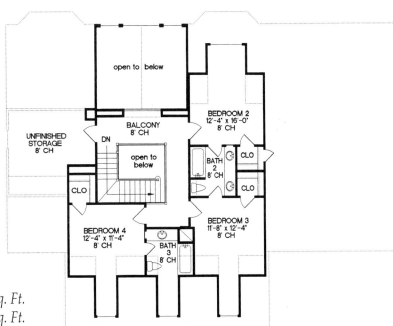

open to below

BEDROOM 2
12'-4" x 16'-0"
8' CH

UNFINISHED
STORAGE
8' CH

BALCONY
8' CH

DN

open to
below

BATH
2
8' CH

CLO

CLO

CLO

BEDROOM 4
12'-4" x 11'-4"
8' CH

BATH
3
8' CH

BEDROOM 3
11'-8" x 12'-4"
8' CH

First Floor	1907 *Sq. Ft.*
Second Floor	908 *Sq. Ft.*
Total Living Area	2815 *Sq. Ft.*

Unfinished Storage adds 171 Sq. Ft.

Ashton Manor

$\mathcal{D}$esigned to take advantage of a unique view, an angled rear porch is joined by French doors from the study and breakfast room. • The visual appeal of this home is best expressed in an eight-sided family room, which offers large rear and side windows, a see-through fireplace, arched entry and two-story ceiling.

Call toll-free
800-947-7526
www.designbasics.com

72

PLAN 9182-9R
price code 28

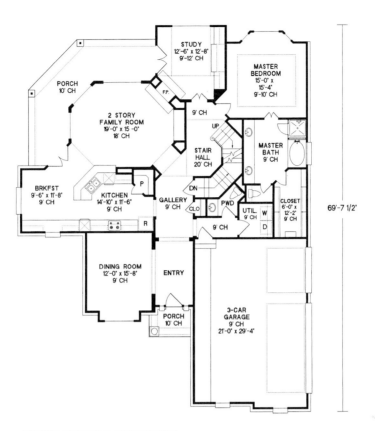

FIRST FLOOR

STUDY
12'-6" x 12'-8"
9'-12' CH

MASTER
BEDROOM
15'-0" x
15'-4"
9'-10' CH

PORCH
10' CH

F.P.

9' CH

2 STORY
FAMILY ROOM
19'-0" x 15'-0"
18' CH

UP

STAIR
HALL
20' CH

MASTER
BATH
9' CH

BRKFST
9'-6" x 11'-8"
9' CH

KITCHEN
14'-10" x 11'-6"
9' CH

P

GALLERY
9' CH

DN

CLO

PWD

UTIL.
9' CH

W
D

CLOSET
6'-0" x
12'-2"
9' CH

R

9' CH

69'-7 1/2"

DINING ROOM
12'-0" x 15'-8"
9' CH

ENTRY

PORCH
10' CH

3-CAR
GARAGE
9' CH
21'-0" x 29'-4"

© CARMICHAEL & DAME DESIGNS, INC.

54'-7"

SECOND FLOOR

2 STORY
FAMILY ROOM
18' CH

20' CH

BEDROOM 4
12'-0" x 11'-0"
8'-11" CH

CLO

BATH
2
8' CH

DN
8' CH

CLOSET
8' CH

BEDROOM 2
13'-2" x 13'-0"
8'-11" CH

8' CH

CLO

BATH
1
8' CH

BEDROOM
3
12'-0" x
14'-0"
8'-11" CH

8' CH

UNFIN.
STORAGE
5'-9' CH

First Floor	1894 Sq. Ft.
Second Floor	936 Sq. Ft.
Total Living Area	**2830 Sq. Ft.**

Unfinished Storage adds 232 Sq. Ft.

*L*ap siding is smartly paired with stone and roof brackets, giving a casual air to the exterior of this home. • An upper-level balcony overlooks the two-story family room with valley cathedral ceiling. • The landing leads to a children's study that's perfect for a home-work area and the family computer.

Call toll-free
800-947-7526
www.designbasics.com

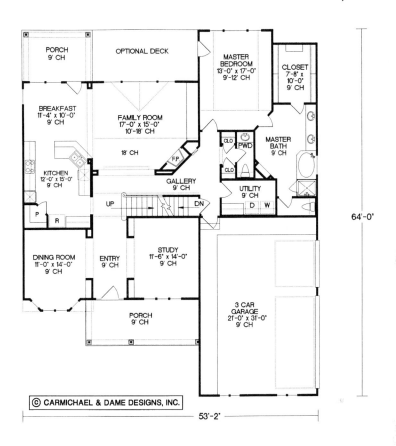

PORCH
9' CH

OPTIONAL DECK

MASTER
BEDROOM
13'-0" x 17'-0"
9'-12' CH

CLOSET
7'-8" x
10'-0"
9' CH

BREAKFAST
11'-4" x 10'-0"
9' CH

FAMILY ROOM
17'-0" x 15'-0"
10'-18' CH

18' CH

FP.

CLO

PWD

MASTER
BATH
9' CH

KITCHEN
12'-0" x 15'-0"
9' CH

CLO

GALLERY
9' CH

UTILITY
9' CH

P   R

UP   DN

D   W

DINING ROOM
11'-0" x 14'-0"
9' CH

ENTRY
9' CH

STUDY
11'-6" x 14'-0"
9' CH

3 CAR
GARAGE
21'-0" x 31'-0"
9' CH

PORCH
9' CH

64'-0"

© CARMICHAEL & DAME DESIGNS, INC.

53'-2"

open to
below

CLO   CLO

CHILDREN'S
STUDY
7'-10" x 12'-0"
8' CH

BRIDGE
8' CH

BEDROOM 4
11'-0" x 12'-0"
8'-10' CH

CLOSET

DN

BATH
3
8' CH

BEDROOM 2
11'-0" x 13'-0"
8'-10' CH

BATH
2
8' CH

CLO

BEDROOM 3
11'-0" x 13'-0"
8' CH

UNFINISHED
STORAGE
5'-8' CH

First Floor	1911 Sq. Ft.
Second Floor	1028 Sq. Ft.
Total Living Area	2939 Sq. Ft.

Unfinished Storage adds 392 Sq. Ft.

Stillwater Court

*O*ld world styling replete with scallops and wing walls characterizes this elegant front elevation. • The living room is visually connected with the dining room and a circular staircase. • Spatial arrangements are even less defined between the kitchen, family room and breakfast area, tied together by a beamed ceiling.

Call toll-free
800-947-7526
www.designbasics.com

PLAN 9167-9R

price code 29

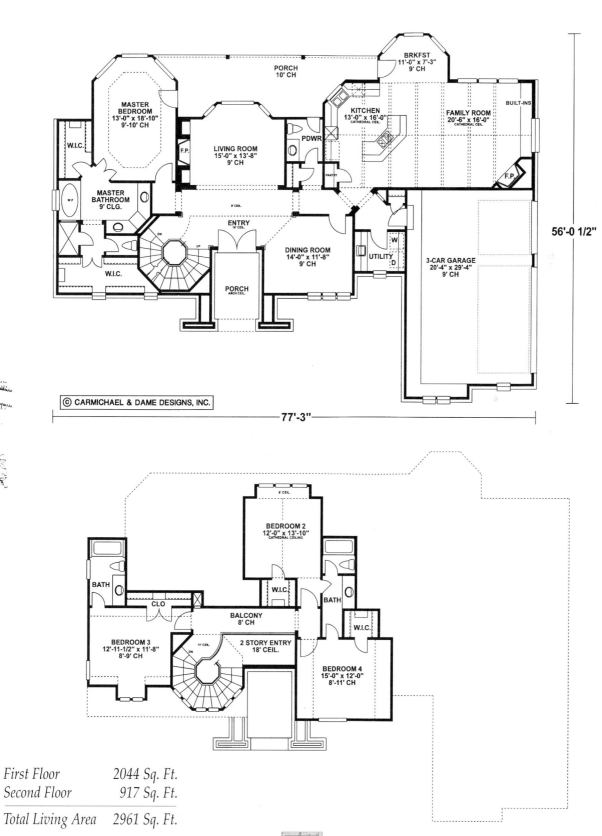

PORCH
10' CH

BRKFST
11'-0" x 7'-3"
9' CH

MASTER
BEDROOM
13'-0" x 18'-10"
9'-10' CH

KITCHEN
13'-0" x 16'-0"
CATHEDRAL CEIL.

FAMILY ROOM
20'-6" x 16'-0"
CATHEDRAL CEIL.

BUILT-INS

W.I.C.

F.P.

LIVING ROOM
15'-0" x 13'-8"
9' CH

PDWR

PANTRY

F.P.

MASTER
BATHROOM
9' CLG.

W P

ENTRY
18' CEIL.

DN

UP

DINING ROOM
14'-0" x 11'-8"
9' CH

UTILITY

W

D

3-CAR GARAGE
20'-4" x 29'-4"
9' CH

W.I.C.

PORCH
ARCH CEIL.

© CARMICHAEL & DAME DESIGNS, INC.

56'-0 1/2"

77'-3"

BEDROOM 2
12'-0" x 13'-10"
CATHEDRAL CEILING

BATH

CLO

W.I.C.

BATH

BEDROOM 3
12'-11-1/2" x 11'-8"
8'-9' CH

BALCONY
8' CH

W.I.C.

DN

2 STORY ENTRY
18' CEIL.

BEDROOM 4
15'-0" x 12'-0"
8'-11' CH

First Floor   2044 Sq. Ft.
Second Floor   917 Sq. Ft.

Total Living Area   2961 Sq. Ft.

Dunhill Manor

$\mathcal{S}$hutters and round pillars perfectly contrast this all-brick front elevation. • Inside, the two-story living room and stairhall share a see-through fireplace. • Together they provide ideal circulation to the study and dining room when entertaining. • The kitchen is set at an angle, with counters determining its U-shape.

Call toll-free
800-947-7526
www.designbasics.com

PLAN 9168-9R

price code 29

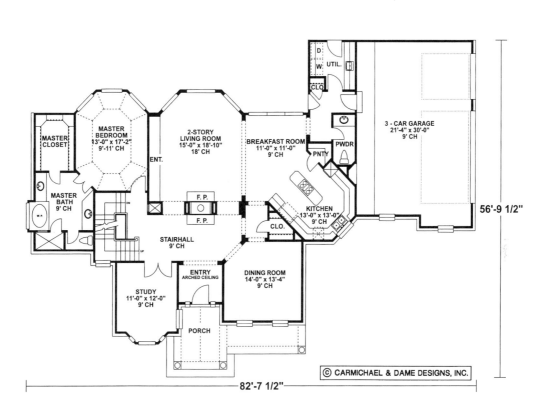

MASTER CLOSET

MASTER BEDROOM
13'-0" x 17'-2"
9'-11' CH

ENT.

2-STORY LIVING ROOM
15'-0" x 18'-10"
18' CH

BREAKFAST ROOM
11'-0" x 11'-0"
9' CH

D
W
UTIL.
CLO

3 - CAR GARAGE
21'-4" x 30'-0"
9' CH

MASTER BATH
9' CH

F. P.

F. P.

PNTY

PWDR

STAIRHALL
9' CH

CLO.

KITCHEN
13'-0" x 13'-0"
9' CH

STUDY
11'-0" x 12'-0"
9' CH

ENTRY
ARCHED CEILING

DINING ROOM
14'-0" x 13'-4"
9' CH

PORCH

56'-9 1/2"

© CARMICHAEL & DAME DESIGNS, INC.

82'-7 1/2"

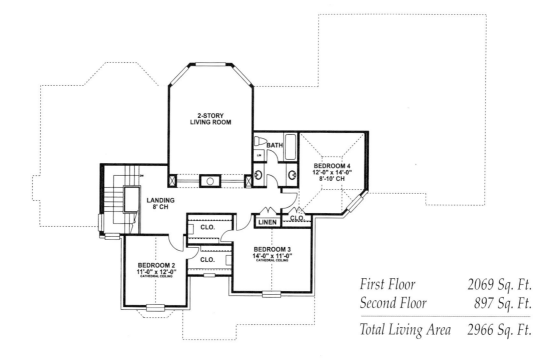

2-STORY LIVING ROOM

BATH

BEDROOM 4
12'-0" x 14'-0"
8'-10' CH

LANDING
8' CH

CLO.

LINEN

CLO.

CLO.

BEDROOM 2
11'-0" x 12'-0"
CATHEDRAL CEILING

BEDROOM 3
14'-0" x 11'-0"
CATHEDRAL CEILING

First Floor	2069 Sq. Ft.
Second Floor	897 Sq. Ft.
Total Living Area	2966 Sq. Ft.

Tealwood Estate

A wrap-around porch adds a pleasant atmosphere to any home, as it certainly does on this elevation. • For added pleasure, both the study and dining room feature French doors that open onto the front porch. • Upstairs, a balcony overlooks the family room and each bedroom has a window seat tucked in a dormer.

Call toll-free
800-947-7526
www.designbasics.com

PLAN 9162-9R
price code 30

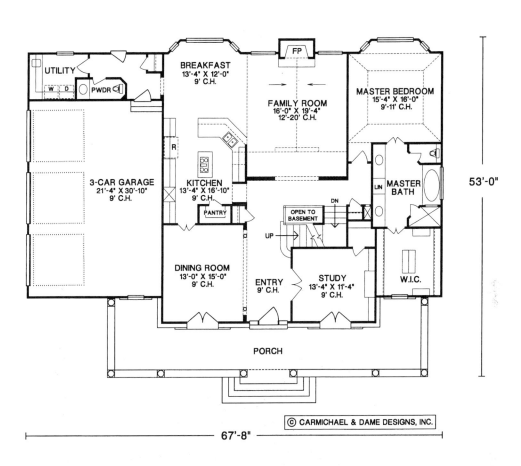

UTILITY

BREAKFAST
13'-4" X 12'-0"
9' C.H.

FP

MASTER BEDROOM
15'-4" X 16'-0"
9'-11" C.H.

FAMILY ROOM
16'-0" X 19'-4"
12'-20' C.H.

W D   PWDR

3-CAR GARAGE
21'-4" X 30'-10"
9' C.H.

R

KITCHEN
13'-4" X 16'-10"
9' C.H.

MASTER
BATH

LIN

PANTRY

OPEN TO
BASEMENT

DN

53'-0"

UP

W.I.C.

DINING ROOM
13'-0" X 15'-0"
9' C.H.

ENTRY
9' C.H.

STUDY
13'-4" X 11'-4"
9' C.H.

PORCH

© CARMICHAEL & DAME DESIGNS, INC.

67'-8"

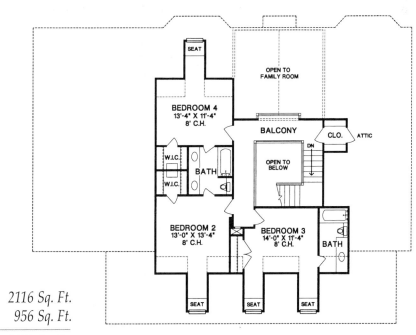

SEAT

OPEN TO
FAMILY ROOM

BEDROOM 4
13'-4" X 11'-4"
8' C.H.

BALCONY

CLO.   ATTIC

W.I.C.

BATH

OPEN TO
BELOW

DN

W.I.C.

BEDROOM 2
13'-0" X 13'-4"
8' C.H.

BEDROOM 3
14'-0" X 11'-4"
8' C.H.

BATH

SEAT   SEAT   SEAT

First Floor   2116 Sq. Ft.
Second Floor   956 Sq. Ft.

Total Living Area   3072 Sq. Ft.

Parkgate Showcase

An expansive roofline is anchored by a front porch and a spray of front-facing windows on the main level. • Interior rooms spin off a central family room offering a fireplace, built-ins and windows towering to a sloped ceiling. • One of those rooms is a study, located midway up the home's U-shaped staircase.

Call toll-free
800-947-7526
www.designbasics.com

PLAN 9181-9R
price code 30

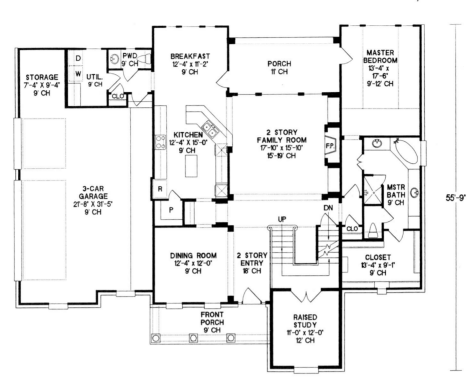

STORAGE
7'-4" X 9'-4"
9' CH

D
W

PWD
9' CH

UTIL.
9' CH

CLO

BREAKFAST
12'-4" x 11'-2"
9' CH

PORCH
11' CH

MASTER
BEDROOM
13'-4" x
17'-6"
9'-12' CH

KITCHEN
12'-4" X 15'-0"
9' CH

2 STORY
FAMILY ROOM
17'-10" x 15'-10"
15'-19' CH

F.P.

3-CAR
GARAGE
21'-8" X 31'-5"
9' CH

R

P

MSTR
BATH
9' CH

55'-9"

UP

DN

CLO

CLOSET
13'-4" x 9'-1"
9' CH

DINING ROOM
12'-4" x 12'-0"
9' CH

2 STORY
ENTRY
18' CH

FRONT
PORCH
9' CH

RAISED
STUDY
11'-0" x 12'-0"
12' CH

© CARMICHAEL & DAME DESIGNS, INC.

68'-3"

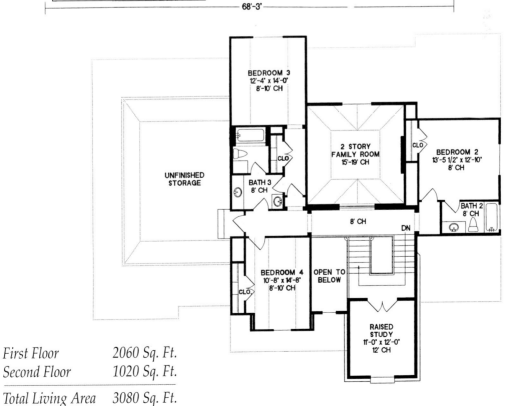

BEDROOM 3
12'-4" x 14'-0"
8'-10' CH

UNFINISHED
STORAGE

CLO

BATH 3
8' CH

2 STORY
FAMILY ROOM
15'-19' CH

CLO

BEDROOM 2
13'-5 1/2" x 12'-10"
8' CH

BATH 2
8' CH

8' CH

DN

BEDROOM 4
10'-8" x 14'-8"
8'-10' CH

CLO

OPEN TO
BELOW

RAISED
STUDY
11'-0" x 12'-0"
12' CH

First Floor   2060 Sq. Ft.
Second Floor   1020 Sq. Ft.

Total Living Area   3080 Sq. Ft.

Unfinished Attic Space adds 493 Sq. Ft.

Kempton Court

*A*n upper-level porch and bayed turret contribute to this home's castle-like demeanor. • Vaulted ceilings bring visual pleasure to the living room, master suite and each upper-level bedroom. • Rear windows, set at varying angles, provide a variety of views.

Call toll-free
800-947-7526
www.designbasics.com

PLAN 9169-9R
price code 30

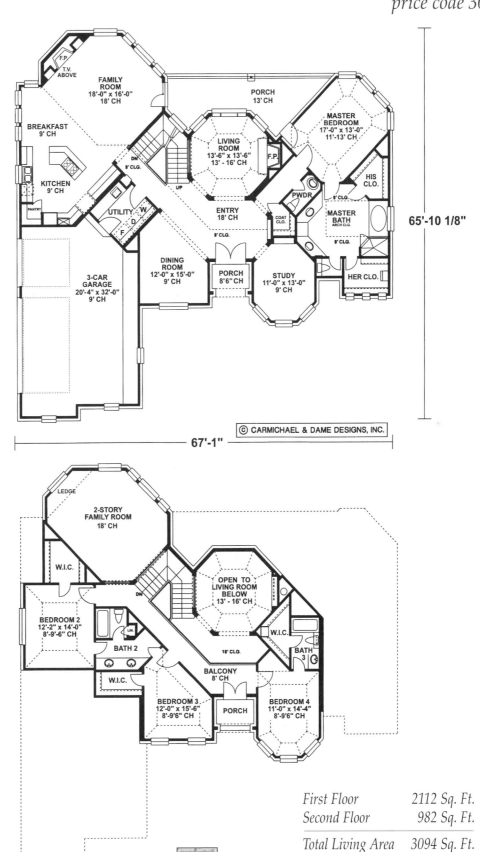

FAMILY ROOM
18'-0" x 16'-0"
18' CH
F.P.
T.V. ABOVE

PORCH
13' CH

MASTER BEDROOM
17'-0" x 13'-0"
11'-13' CH

BREAKFAST
9' CH

LIVING ROOM
13'-6" x 13'-6"
13' - 16' CH

F.P.

DN
8' CLG.
UP

HIS CLO.
8' CLG.

KITCHEN
9' CH

PANTRY

UTILITY
W
D
F

ENTRY
18' CH

COAT CLO.
8' CLG.

PWDR

MASTER BATH
ARCH CLG.
8' CLG.

3-CAR GARAGE
20'-4" x 32'-0"
9' CH

DINING ROOM
12'-0" x 15'-0"
9' CH

PORCH
8'6" CH

STUDY
11'-0" x 13'-0"
9' CH

HER CLO.

65'-10 1/8"

© CARMICHAEL & DAME DESIGNS, INC.

67'-1"

LEDGE

2-STORY FAMILY ROOM
18' CH

W.I.C.

DN

OPEN TO LIVING ROOM BELOW
13' - 16' CH

W.I.C.

BEDROOM 2
12'-2" x 14'-0"
8'-9'-6" CH

LIN.

BATH 2

BATH 3

W.I.C.

BALCONY
8' CH

18' CLG.

W.I.C.

BEDROOM 3
12'-0" x 15'-6"
8'-9'6" CH

PORCH

BEDROOM 4
11'-0" x 14'-4"
8'-9'6" CH

First Floor	2112 Sq. Ft.
Second Floor	982 Sq. Ft.
Total Living Area	3094 Sq. Ft.

As almost everyone knows, two-story homes are the most economical of designs, and often the most predictable. The two-story designs of Carmichael & Dame, however, are anything but typical. As with all of their designs, Dame took special care to bring light into a variety of spaces. The number and, sometimes, unusual placement of windows generates excitement on the exterior. Stair halls are of particular importance in the two-story designs on the following pages. It's there that Dame visually connects the upper level with the main level through the use of two-story ceilings, balconies and stairwall windows. The staircases are always visually appealing themselves, enticing one to climb and explore the upper level.

Two-Story *Homes*

Plan #	Plan Name	Sq. Ft.	Page #
9192	Tuscany House	1747	88-89
9202	Riveria Court	1835	90-91
9176	Baldwin Court	2042	92-93
9197	Eldridge Court	2363	94-95
9172	Bibury Manor	2438	96-97
9204	Amherst Estate	2523	98-99
9177	Pebble Brook	2630	100-101
9186	Wilcrest Court	2688	102-103
9184	Rivercrest Manor	2705	104-105
9161	Woodvine Manor	2715	106-107
9163	Cambridge Court	3222	108-109

Tuscany House

An entry tower on this elevation is adorned with board-on-board shutters and roof brackets. • Inside, bayed windows in the family room overlook a rear porch that joins the dining area. • A bedroom is secluded on the main level for a guest or live-in relative.

Call toll-free
800-947-7526
www.designbasics.com

PLAN 9192-9R

price code 17

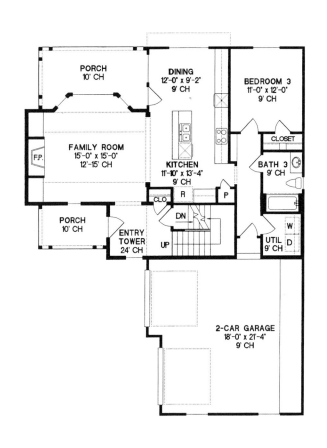

PORCH
10' CH

DINING
12'-0" x 9'-2"
9' CH

BEDROOM 3
11'-0" x 12'-0"
9' CH

CLOSET

FAMILY ROOM
15'-0" x 15'-0"
12'-15' CH

F.P.

KITCHEN
11'-10" x 13'-4"
9' CH

BATH 3
9' CH

CLO.

R

P

DN

PORCH
10' CH

ENTRY
TOWER
24' CH

UP

UTIL
9' CH

W

D

2-CAR GARAGE
18'-0" x 21'-4"
9' CH

55'-6"

42'-0"

© CARMICHAEL & DAME DESIGNS, INC.

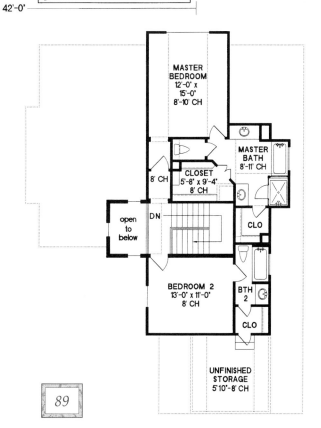

MASTER
BEDROOM
12'-0" x
15'-0"
8'-10' CH

MASTER
BATH
8'-11' CH

CLOSET
5'-8" x 9'-4"
8' CH

8' CH

CLO

open
to
below

DN

CLO

BEDROOM 2
13'-0" x 11'-0"
8' CH

BTH
2

UNFINISHED
STORAGE
5'10"-8' CH

CUSTOMIZE
any home plan

First Floor   1040 Sq. Ft.
Second Floor   707 Sq. Ft.

Total Living Area   1747 Sq. Ft.

Unfinished Storage adds 140 Sq. Ft.

This traditional farmhouse is given a new look with front-facing gables and a copper roof. • A U-shaped staircase offers beauty in the entry and leads to an upper-level balcony that takes in the family room. • A cathedral ceiling marks the master suite, which features vanities for him and her, a whirlpool tub and walk-in closet with built-ins.

Call toll-free
800-947-7526
www.designbasics.com

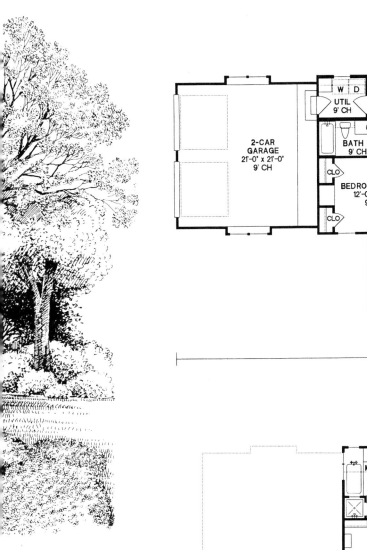

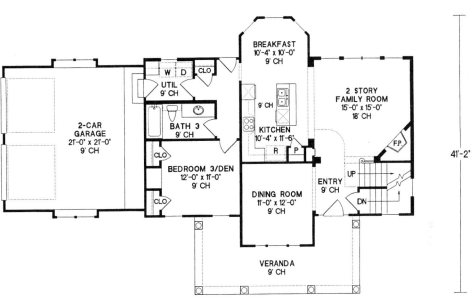

BREAKFAST
10'-4" x 10'-0"
9' CH

2 STORY
FAMILY ROOM
15'-0" x 15'-0"
18' CH

W D

CLO

UTIL
9' CH

9' CH

KITCHEN
10'-4" x 11'-6"

FP.

BATH 3
9' CH

R P

2-CAR
GARAGE
21'-0" x 21'-0"
9' CH

CLO

BEDROOM 3/DEN
12'-0" x 11'-0"
9' CH

DINING ROOM
11'-0" x 12'-0"
9' CH

ENTRY
9' CH

UP

CLO

DN

VERANDA
9' CH

41'-2"

63'-2"

© CARMICHAEL & DAME DESIGNS, INC.

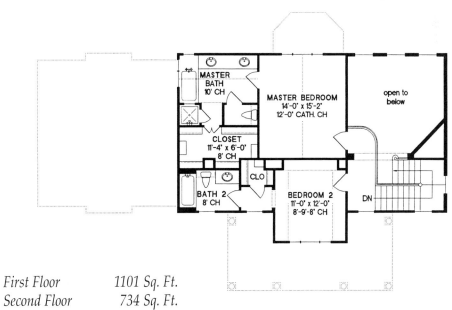

MASTER
BATH
10' CH

MASTER BEDROOM
14'-0" x 15'-2"
12'-0" CATH. CH

open to
below

CLOSET
11'-4" x 6'-0"
8' CH

CLO

BATH 2
8' CH

BEDROOM 2
11'-0" x 12'-0"
8'-9'-8" CH

DN

First Floor	*1101 Sq. Ft.*
Second Floor	*734 Sq. Ft.*
Total Living Area	*1835 Sq. Ft.*

Baldwin Court

The long patterns repeated in this home's roofline, accentuate to its two-story design. • All bedrooms are located on the upper level - each with distinctive ceilings for visual pleasure. • Dormers bring light into a large attic that allows expansion or a place for storage.

Call toll-free
800-947-7526
www.designbasics.com

PLAN 9176-9R
price code 20

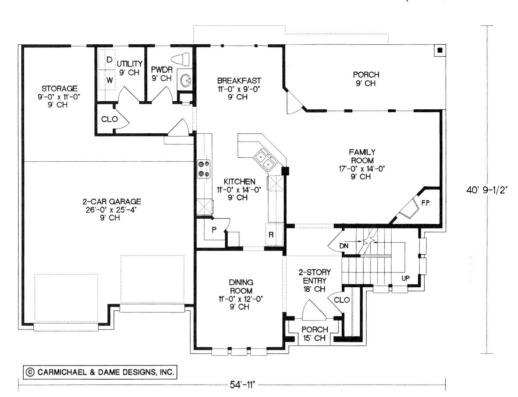

STORAGE
9'-0" x 11'-0"
9' CH

D
W

UTILITY
9' CH

PWDR
9' CH

CLO

BREAKFAST
11'-0" x 9'-0"
9' CH

PORCH
9' CH

KITCHEN
11'-0" x 14'-0"
9' CH

FAMILY
ROOM
17'-0" x 14'-0"
9' CH

F.P.

2-CAR GARAGE
26'-0" x 25'-4"
9' CH

P

R

DN

UP

40' 9-1/2"

DINING
ROOM
11'-0" x 12'-0"
9' CH

2-STORY
ENTRY
18' CH

CLO

PORCH
15' CH

© CARMICHAEL & DAME DESIGNS, INC.

54'-11"

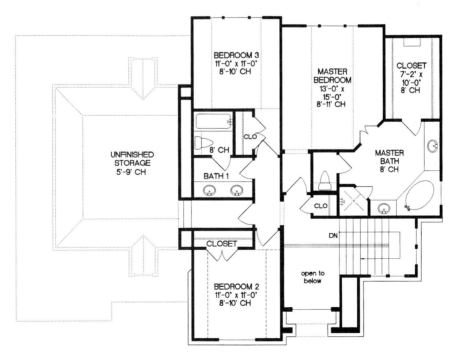

UNFINISHED
STORAGE
5'-9' CH

BEDROOM 3
11'-0" x 11'-0"
8'-10' CH

MASTER
BEDROOM
13'-0" x
15'-0"
8'-11' CH

CLOSET
7'-2" x
10'-0"
8' CH

8' CH

CLO

BATH 1

MASTER
BATH
8' CH

CLO

DN.

CLOSET

open to
below

BEDROOM 2
11'-0" x 11'-0"
8'-10' CH

First Floor   1063 Sq. Ft.
Second Floor   979 Sq. Ft.

Total Living Area   2042 Sq. Ft.

Unfinished Storage adds 352 Sq. Ft.

Eldridge Court

A copper-clad roof and stacked square windows are refreshing features on this facade. • A wrap-around porch leads inside, where a light-filled staircase leads to four upper-level bedrooms. • French doors blur the lines between the kitchen and rear porch, offering ideal circulation and entertainment options.

Call toll-free
800-947-7526
www.designbasics.com

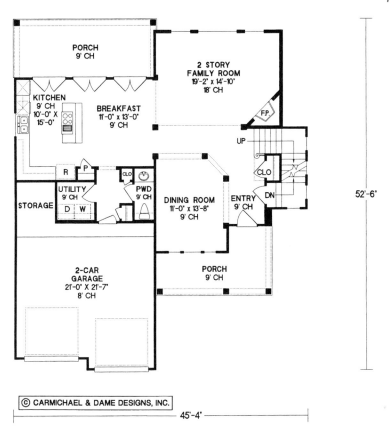

PORCH
9' CH

2 STORY
FAMILY ROOM
19'-2" x 14'-10"
18' CH

KITCHEN
9' CH
10'-0" X
15'-0"

BREAKFAST
11'-0" x 13'-0"
9' CH

F.P.

UP

R   P

CLO

CLO

UTILITY
9' CH

PWD
9' CH

DINING ROOM
11'-0" x 13'-8"
9' CH

ENTRY
9' CH

DN

STORAGE

D   W

2-CAR
GARAGE
21'-0" X 21'-7"
8' CH

PORCH
9' CH

52'-6"

© CARMICHAEL & DAME DESIGNS, INC.

45'-4"

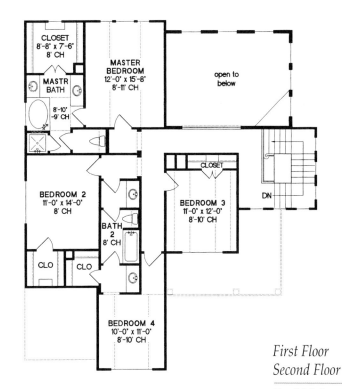

CLOSET
8'-8" x 7'-6"
8' CH

MASTER
BEDROOM
12'-0" x 15'-8"
8'-11' CH

open to
below

MASTR
BATH

8'-10"
-9' CH

BEDROOM 2
11'-0" x 14'-0"
8' CH

CLOSET

BEDROOM 3
11'-0" x 12'-0"
8'-10' CH

DN

BATH
2
8' CH

CLO   CLO

BEDROOM 4
10'-0" x 11'-0"
8'-10' CH

First Floor	1105 Sq. Ft.
Second Floor	1258 Sq. Ft.
Total Living Area	2363 Sq. Ft.

Bibury Manor

*T*he inclusion of shutters and brackets softens this home's brick facade. • The dining room is immediately visible in the entry. • A rear porch adds living space to the home.

Call toll-free
800-947-7526
www.designbasics.com

PLAN 9172-9R
price code 24

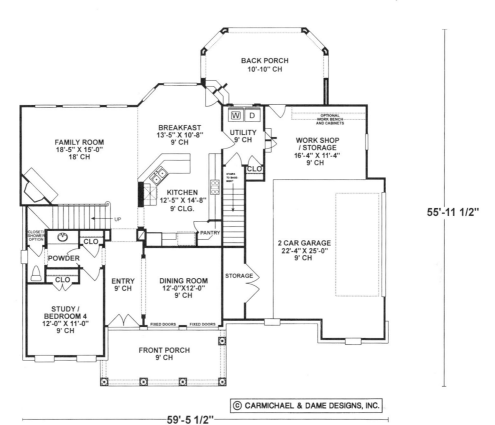

BACK PORCH
10'-10" CH

FAMILY ROOM
18'-5" X 15'-0"
18' CH

BREAKFAST
13'-5" X 10'-8"
9' CH

UTILITY
9' CH

W   D

OPTIONAL
WORK BENCH
AND CABINETS

WORK SHOP
/ STORAGE
16'-4" X 11'-4"
9' CH

CLO

KITCHEN
12'-5" X 14'-8"
9' CLG.

STAIRS
TO BASE-
MENT

UP

CLOSET/
SHOWER
OPTION

CLO

PANTRY

55'-11 1/2"

POWDER

CLO

ENTRY
9' CH

DINING ROOM
12'-0"X12'-0"
9' CH

STORAGE

2 CAR GARAGE
22'-4" X 25'-0"
9' CH

STUDY /
BEDROOM 4
12'-0" X 11'-0"
9' CH

FIXED DOORS   FIXED DOORS

FRONT PORCH
9' CH

© CARMICHAEL & DAME DESIGNS, INC.

59'-5 1/2"

OPEN TO
BELOW

MASTER
BEDROOM
13'-0" X 17'-0"
8'-11' CH

MASTER
BATH
8' CH

MASTER
CLOSET
8' CH

LEDGE

DOWN

BALCONY
8' CH

LADDER

OPTIONAL ATTIC
8' CH

CLO   CLO

CLO.

ATTIC
ACCESS

BEDROOM 3
12'-4" X 11'-4"
10' CH

BATH 2
8' CH

BEDROOM 2
13'-0" X 12'-0"
8' CH

8' CH

First Floor   1280 Sq. Ft.
Second Floor   1158 Sq. Ft.

Total Living Area   2438 Sq. Ft.

Unfinished Attic Space adds 285 Sq. Ft.

Amherst Estate

$\mathcal{D}$ecorative roof brackets make a statement on this uniquely stacked elevation. • Whether from the front or rear of the home, a T-shaped staircase allows access to the upper level. • The family room features a library alcove, granting a quiet haven for conversation. • To the rear, a porch offers a second retreat.

PLAN 9204-9R
price code 25

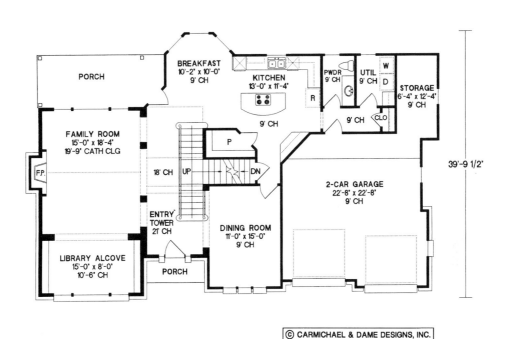

PORCH

BREAKFAST
10'-2" x 10'-0"
9' CH

KITCHEN
13'-0" x 11'-4"

PWDR
9' CH

UTIL
9' CH

W
D

STORAGE
6'-4" x 12'-4"
9' CH

FAMILY ROOM
15'-0" x 18'-4"
19'-9" CATH CLG

9' CH

CLO
9' CH

F.P.

18' CH

UP

DN

P

2-CAR GARAGE
22'-8" x 22'-8"
9' CH

39'-9 1/2"

ENTRY
TOWER
21' CH

DINING ROOM
11'-0" x 15'-0"
9' CH

LIBRARY ALCOVE
15'-0" x 8'-0"
10'-6" CH

PORCH

© CARMICHAEL & DAME DESIGNS, INC.

64'-1 1/2"

open to
below

MASTER
BEDROOM
13'-0" x 15'-0"
8'-11" CH

MASTER BATH
8' - 10'6" CH

CLOSET
10'-6" x 7'-4"
8' CH

18' CH

DN

8' CH

CLO

8' CH

BATH
2

CLOSET

CLOSET

CLOSET

BEDROOM
2
11'-0" x 12'-8"
8'-10" CH

BEDROOM
3
11'-4" x 10'-8"
8' CH

BEDROOM
4
11'-0" x 11'-0"
10' CH

First Floor   1373 Sq. Ft.
Second Floor   1150 Sq. Ft.

Total Living Area   2523 Sq. Ft.

Call toll-free
800-947-7526
www.designbasics.com

99

Tightly spaced windows joined with shutters offer a visual welcome into this home. • These windows light a three-car garage, study, the master suite and an upper-level computer alcove. • Nine-foot ceilings further stretch the spacious appeal of all upper-level rooms.

Call toll-free
800-947-7526
www.designbasics.com

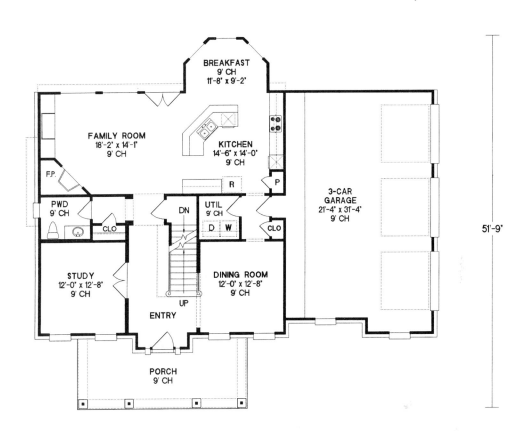

BREAKFAST
9' CH
11'-8" x 9'-2"

FAMILY ROOM
18'-2" x 14'-1"
9' CH

KITCHEN
14'-6" x 14'-0"
9' CH

3-CAR
GARAGE
21'-4" x 31'-4"
9' CH

F.P.

PWD
9' CH

CLO

DN

UTIL
9' CH

R

P

CLO

D W

51'-9"

STUDY
12'-0" x 12'-8"
9' CH

DINING ROOM
12'-0" x 12'-8"
9' CH

ENTRY

UP

PORCH
9' CH

© CARMICHAEL & DAME DESIGNS, INC.

59'-1 1/2"

CLOSET
9'-0" x 7'-0"
9' CH

BEDROOM 4
11'-0" x 11'-0"
9' CH

BEDROOM 3
11'-8" x 12'-1"
9' CH

CLO

MASTER
BATH
9' CH

CLO

CLO
9' CH

9' CH

UNFINISHED
STORAGE
5'-9" CH

DN

BATH 1
9' CH

CLO

MASTER
BEDROOM
12'-0" x
15'-8"
9'-11" CH

BEDROOM 2
12'-2" x 11'-4"
9' CH

COMPUTER
ALCOVE
10'-6" CH

First Floor   1285 Sq. Ft.
Second Floor   1345 Sq. Ft.

Total Living Area   2630 Sq. Ft.

Unfinished Storage adds 352 Sq. Ft.

Wilcrest Court

*E*nter this home either through the front covered stoop or its spacious courtyard with fountain. • A secluded study offers a great place to work out of the home. • The staircase leads to a mid-level landing that accesses potential storage space above the garage. • A romantic window and tall ceiling showcase the master bath's whirlpool tub.

Call toll-free
800-947-7526
www.designbasics.com

PLAN 9186-9R
price code 26

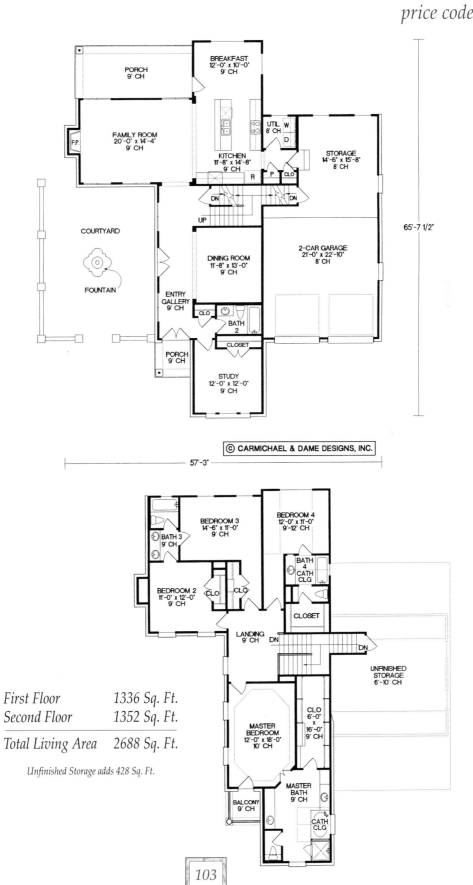

PORCH 9' CH

BREAKFAST 12'-0" x 10'-0" 9' CH

FAMILY ROOM 20'-0" x 14'-4" 9' CH

F.P.

KITCHEN 11'-8" x 14'-8" 9' CH

UTIL 8' CH W D

STORAGE 14'-6" x 15'-8" 8' CH

CLO R P CLO

DN DN

UP

COURTYARD

FOUNTAIN

DINING ROOM 11'-8" x 13'-0" 9' CH

2-CAR GARAGE 21'-0" x 22'-10" 8' CH

ENTRY GALLERY 9' CH

CLO **BATH 2**

PORCH 9' CH

CLOSET

STUDY 12'-0" x 12'-0" 9' CH

65'-7 1/2'

© CARMICHAEL & DAME DESIGNS, INC.

57'-3'

BEDROOM 3 14'-6" x 11'-0" 9' CH

BEDROOM 4 12'-0" x 11'-0" 9'-12' CH

BATH 3 9' CH

BEDROOM 2 11'-0" x 12'-0" 9' CH

CLO CLO

BATH 4 CATH CLG

CLOSET

LANDING 9' CH DN DN

UNFINISHED STORAGE 6'-10' CH

MASTER BEDROOM 12'-0" x 18'-0" 10' CH

CLO 6'-0" x 16'-0" 9' CH

BALCONY 9' CH

MASTER BATH 9' CH

CATH CLG

First Floor   1336 Sq. Ft.
Second Floor   1352 Sq. Ft.
─────────────────────────────────
Total Living Area   2688 Sq. Ft.

Unfinished Storage adds 428 Sq. Ft.

Rivercrest Manor

The expanse of a double gable hides the separation of a second garage. • The seclusion of the study is contrasted by triple front and rear windows. • An island counter with sink and eating bar is positioned to include the rear porch as entertaining, eating and living space.

Call toll-free
800-947-7526
www.designbasics.com

PLAN 9184-9R
price code 27

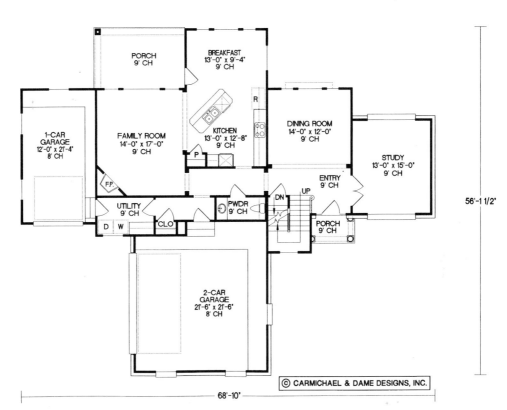

PORCH
9' CH

BREAKFAST
13'-0" x 9'-4"
9' CH

1-CAR
GARAGE
12'-0" x 21'-4"
8' CH

FAMILY ROOM
14'-0" x 17'-0"
9' CH

KITCHEN
13'-0" x 12'-8"
9' CH

DINING ROOM
14'-0" x 12'-0"
9' CH

STUDY
13'-0" x 15'-0"
9' CH

FP.

UTILITY
9' CH

CLO

PWDR
9' CH

DN

UP

ENTRY
9' CH

PORCH
9' CH

D   W

2-CAR
GARAGE
21'-6" x 21'-6"
8' CH

© CARMICHAEL & DAME DESIGNS, INC.

56'-1 1/2"

68'-10"

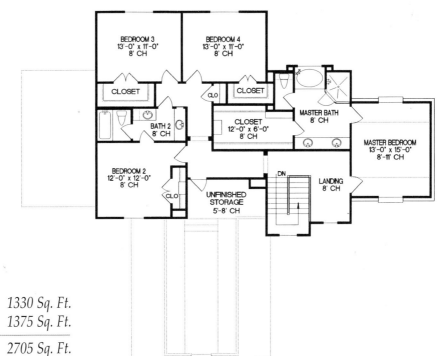

BEDROOM 3
13'-0" x 11'-0"
8' CH

BEDROOM 4
13'-0" x 11'-0"
8' CH

CLOSET

CLO

CLOSET

MASTER BATH
8' CH

BATH 2
8' CH

CLOSET
12'-0" x 6'-0"
8' CH

MASTER BEDROOM
13'-0" x 15'-0"
8'-11' CH

BEDROOM 2
12'-0" x 12'-0"
8' CH

CLO

UNFINISHED
STORAGE
5'-8' CH

DN

LANDING
8' CH

First Floor	*1330 Sq. Ft.*
Second Floor	*1375 Sq. Ft.*
Total Living Area	*2705 Sq. Ft.*

Unfinished Storage adds 346 Sq. Ft.

Woodvine Manor

The main floor design of this home reveals itself in a natural U shape, with formal rooms giving way to the everyday living areas. • A sunken location provides a bit of drama for the master bath. • It includes his-and-her walk-in closets, vanities and a whirlpool tub under a window.

Call toll-free
800-947-7526
www.designbasics.com

PLAN 9161-9R

price code 27

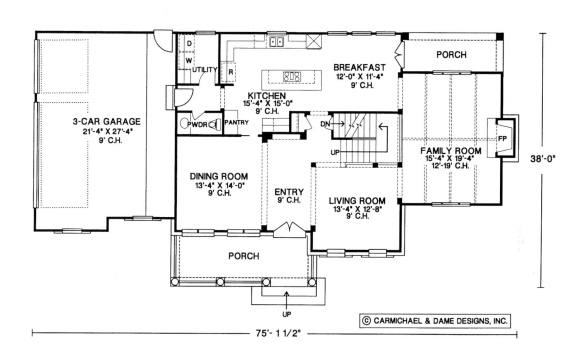

3-CAR GARAGE
21'-4" X 27'-4"
9' C.H.

PORCH

D
W
UTILITY
R

BREAKFAST
12'-0" X 11'-4"
9' C.H.

KITCHEN
15'-4" X 15'-0"
9' C.H.

PWDR
PANTRY

DN
UP

FAMILY ROOM
15'-4" X 19'-4"
12'-19' C.H.

FP

38'-0"

DINING ROOM
13'-4" X 14'-0"
9' C.H.

ENTRY
9' C.H.

LIVING ROOM
13'-4" X 12'-8"
9' C.H.

PORCH

UP

© CARMICHAEL & DAME DESIGNS, INC.

75'- 1 1/2"

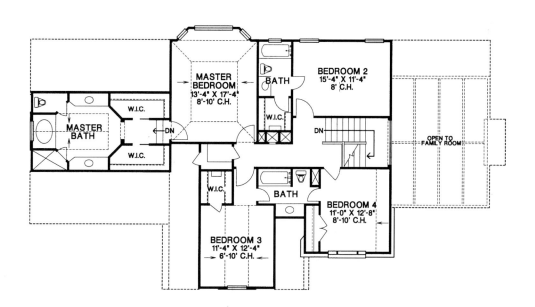

MASTER BATH

W.I.C.
W.I.C.

MASTER BEDROOM
13'-4" X 17'-4"
8'-10' C.H.

BATH

W.I.C.

BEDROOM 2
15'-4" X 11'-4"
8' C.H.

DN

DN

OPEN TO FAMILY ROOM

W.I.C.

BATH

BEDROOM 4
11'-0" X 12'-8"
8'-10' C.H.

BEDROOM 3
11'-4" X 12'-4"
6'-10' C.H.

CUSTOMIZE
any home plan

First Floor	*1400 Sq. Ft.*
Second Floor	*1315 Sq. Ft.*
Total Living Area	*2715 Sq. Ft.*

Cambridge Court

This home is reminiscent of an English Cottage, with stone exterior and double doors trimmed with iron hinges. • There are two especially notable aspects inside: a spacious entry with the dining room and living room separated by symmetrically placed arches, and an upper-level reading loft that overlooks the family room.

Call toll-free
800-947-7526
www.designbasics.com

PLAN 9163-9R

price code 32

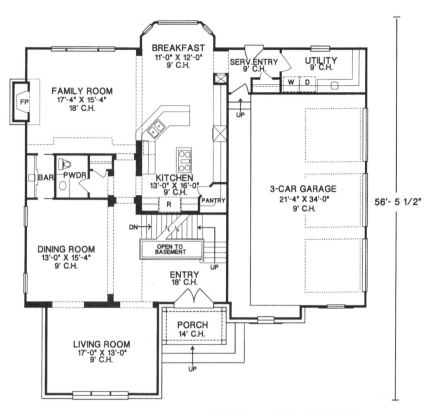

BREAKFAST
11'-0" X 12'-0"
9' C.H.

SERV. ENTRY
9' C.H.

UTILITY
9' C.H.

W D

FAMILY ROOM
17'-4" X 15'-4"
18' C.H.

FP

UP

BAR

PWDR

KITCHEN
13'-0" X 16'-0"
9' C.H.

R

PANTRY

3-CAR GARAGE
21'-4" X 34'-0"
9' C.H.

56'- 5 1/2"

DINING ROOM
13'-0" X 15'-4"
9' C.H.

DN

OPEN TO BASEMENT

UP

ENTRY
18' C.H.

LIVING ROOM
17'-0" X 13'-0"
9' C.H.

PORCH
14' C.H.

UP

© CARMICHAEL & DAME DESIGNS, INC.

— 55'- 9 1/2" —

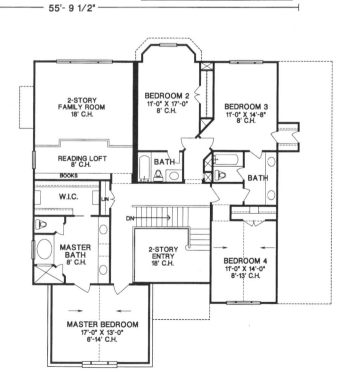

2-STORY FAMILY ROOM
18' C.H.

BEDROOM 2
11'-0" X 17'-0"
8' C.H.

BEDROOM 3
11'-0" X 14'-8"
8' C.H.

READING LOFT
8' C.H.

BOOKS

BATH

BATH

W.I.C.

LIN

DN

MASTER BATH
8' C.H.

2-STORY ENTRY
18' C.H.

BEDROOM 4
11'-0" X 14'-0"
8'-13' C.H.

MASTER BEDROOM
17'-0" X 13'-0"
6'-14' C.H.

First Floor	1655 Sq. Ft.
Second Floor	1567 Sq. Ft.
Total Living Area	3222 Sq. Ft.

Timeless *Legacy*™

The following ten designs, originally published in the Timeless Legacy™ Collection were included in this book to give a sampling of some larger designs from Carmichael & Dame. The homes' stately exteriors and impressive interiors are a natural fit with the newest designs from Carmichael & Dame. Each offers an abundance of natural light and takes advantage of the views to the outside. Public and private spaces appropriately blend for family activities, entertaining or time alone. Each design features a luxurious master suite – with amenities that beckon one to unwind at the end of the day. And true to every Carmichael & Dame design, each was carefully crafted to maintain the home's original character, making each home a unique expression of those who build it.

Special Offer!

THE TIMELESS LEGACY™ COLLECTION

CAN NOW BE YOURS FOR ONLY

$9⁹⁵

CALL 800-947-7526

AND ASK FOR OFFER 9R

CARMICHAEL & DAME DESIGNS

The Whitmore

PLAN 9120-9R
price code 33

The Belle Mede

PLAN 9121-9R
price code 33

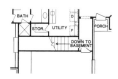

Optional Basement Access

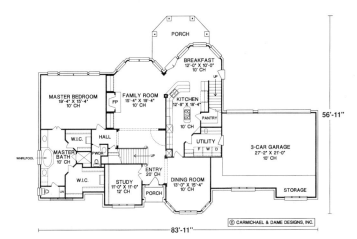

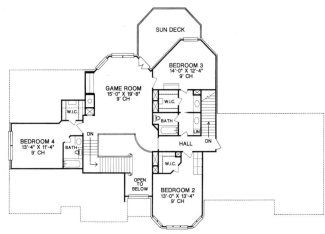

Total Living Area   3312 Sq. Ft.

Call toll-free
800-947-7526
www.designbasics.com

First Floor   2117 Sq. Ft.
Second Floor   1206 Sq. Ft.
_____
Total Living Area   3323 Sq. Ft.

Optional Basement Access

Drakewood Manor
PLAN 9138-9R
price code 33

Claridge House
PLAN 9157-9R
price code 35

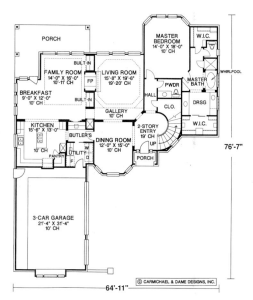

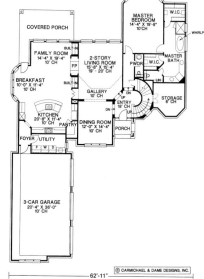

Call toll-free
800-947-7526
www.designbasics.com

First Floor	2050 Sq. Ft.
Second Floor	1467 Sq. Ft.
Total Living Area	3517 Sq. Ft.

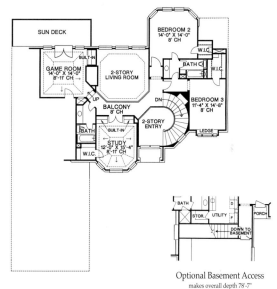

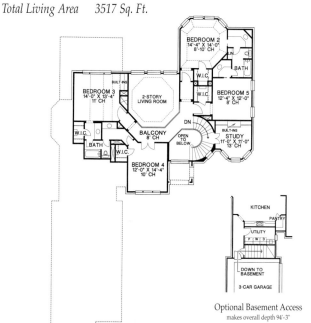

Optional Basement Access
makes overall depth 78'-7"

First Floor	2144 Sq. Ft.
Second Floor	1253 Sq. Ft.
Total Living Area	3397 Sq. Ft.

Optional Basement Access
makes overall depth 94'-3"

Weybridge Manor
PLAN 9128-9R
price code 35

Medinah Manor
PLAN 9147-9R
price code 36

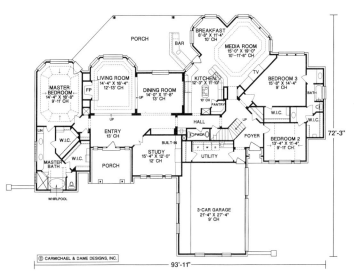

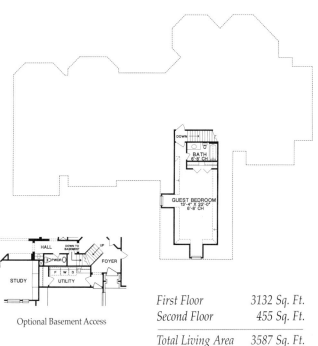

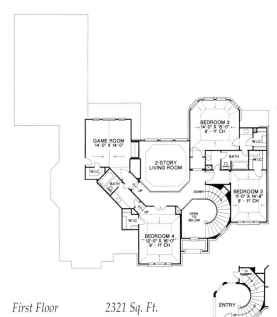

Optional Basement Access

First Floor	3132 Sq. Ft.
Second Floor	455 Sq. Ft.
Total Living Area	3587 Sq. Ft.

First Floor	2321 Sq. Ft.
Second Floor	1356 Sq. Ft.
Total Living Area	3677 Sq. Ft.

Optional Basement Access

Wingham Court
PLAN 9115-9R
price code 36

Meadowview Manor
PLAN 9114-9R
price code 41

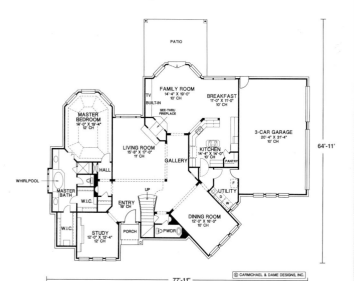

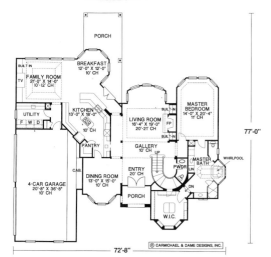

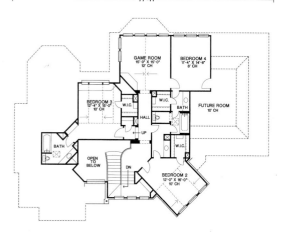

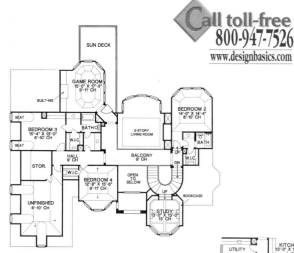

Call toll-free
800-947-7526
www.designbasics.com

First Floor	2362 Sq. Ft.
Second Floor	1319 Sq. Ft.
Total Living Area	3681 Sq. Ft.

Unfinished Future Space adds 301 Sq. Ft.

First Floor	2489 Sq. Ft.
Second Floor	1650 Sq. Ft.
Total Living Area	4139 Sq. Ft.

Unfinished Storage adds 233 Sq. Ft.

Optional Basement Access
makes overall depth 82'-3"

Optional Basement Access
makes overall depth 81'-0"

Sweetwater Bend
PLAN 9119-9R
price code 42

Westleton Manor
PLAN 9133-9R
price code 45

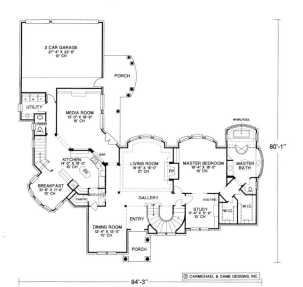

© CARMICHAEL & DAME DESIGNS, INC.

84'-3"

80'-1"

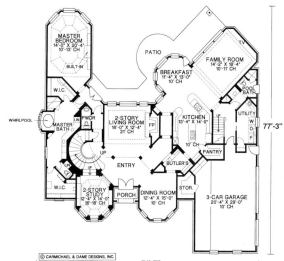

© CARMICHAEL & DAME DESIGNS, INC.

74'-7"

77'-3"

Call toll-free
800-947-7526
www.designbasics.com

First Floor   2688 Sq. Ft.
Second Floor   1540 Sq. Ft.

Total Living Area   4228 Sq. Ft.

Unfinished Storage adds 184 Sq. Ft.

Optional Basement Access

First Floor   2897 Sq. Ft.
Second Floor   1603 Sq. Ft.

Total Living Area   4500 Sq. Ft.

Optional Basement Access

Every plan CAN BE CUSTOMIZED

CUSTOMIZE
any home plan

If one of these designs is *almost* what you want, **Carmichael & Dame** will make it *exactly* what you want.

For information on any custom changes,

Call (800) 947-7526

www.designbasics.com

COPYRIGHT
Cans & Cannots

ALL PLANS HAVE BEEN REGISTERED
ORIGINAL
C
DRAFT
WITH THE U.S. COPYRIGHT OFFICE

These days it seems almost everybody has a question about what can or cannot be done with copyrighted home plans. We know U.S. copyright law can sometimes get complex and confusing, but here are a few of the basic points of the law you'll want to remember. Once you've purchased a plan from us and have received a construction license

You Can . . .

- Construct the plan as originally designed, or change it to meet your specific needs.
- Build it as many times as you wish *without* additional re-use fees.
- Make duplicate blueprint copies as needed for construction.

You Cannot . . .

- Build your plans without a construction license.
- Copy *any* part of our original designs to create another design of your own.
- Claim copyright on changes you make to our plans.
- Give a plan to someone else for construction purposes.
- Sell the plan.

PROTECT YOUR RIGHTS to build, modify and reproduce our home plans with a construction license.

The above points are provided as general guidelines only. Additional information is provided with each home plan purchase, or is available upon request at (800) 947-7526.

There's always something
new going on at Design Basics

Visit Our Website Today!

design basics inc® HOME PLAN DESIGN SERVICE (800) 947-7526 FAX:(402)331-5507

WELCOME TO AMERICA'S #1 HOME PLAN DESIGN SERVICE

Award-winning Designs

Browse hundreds of our award-winning designs with our easy-to-use online search engine.

Monthly Designs

Each month we showcase a design from each of our collections.

DBI Builders

Visit builders in your state who have linked their websites to Design Basics.

Plan Books

Check out our complete library of home design books.

What's New

Find out about new plans and products from Design Basics.

Newspaper Syndication

We now offer an online "Home of the Week" syndication feature that your local newspaper can download and use for free. Make sure you let them know.

Industry Links

Potential buyers can visit your site. We receive over **two million** hits per month. You can't afford *not* to be here.

Construction Alternatives

Discover the possibilities of panelized construction.

Common Questions

Find answers to the most commonly asked questions about our designs.

TO SEE THIS HOME OR OTHER HOME PLANS, VISIT US AT:

www.designbasics.com
E-mail: info@designbasics.com

Space Planning PRODUCTS & SERVICES

Great Ways to Simplify Your Life

For many home buyers, visualizing the finished home is a challenge. Our Study Print & Furniture Layout Guide™ makes it easy. First, the **Study Print provides views of all exterior elevations.** Secondly, the **Furniture Layout Guide provides a "Feel" for room sizes,** with a ¼" scale floor plan, over 100 reusable furniture pieces and helpful tips on space planning.

– Available for most plans –

only $29.95

STUDY PRINT & FURNITURE LAYOUT GUIDE™

Specifications & Finishing
CHECKLIST™

With this handy **reference tool** you'll never forget the little things. Each decision you need to make during the construction of your home is outlined in an easy-to-follow format. Everything from the types of excavation to the brand and style of doorknobs.

No builder or consumer should be without the Specifications & Finishing Checklist™ from Design Basics.

18" x 24" Format

CHOOSE EITHER FORMAT

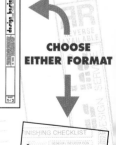

8½" x 11" Format

Call 800|947|7526 To Order

$14.95 EACH

9R

DESIGN BASICS' HOME PLAN LIBRARY

16.

17.

1. **2.**

1) Impressions of Home™
Homes designed with the **look you want** – 100 designs from 1339' to 4139'. $4.95

2) Impressions of Home™
Homes designed for **the way you live** – 100 designs from 1191' to 4228'. $4.95

3) Heartland Home Plans™
120 plan ideas designed for everyday practicality. Warm, unpretentious elevations easily adapt to individual lifestyles. From 1212' to 2631'. $8.95

4) Reflections of an American Home™ Vol. III
50 photographed home plans with warm remembrances of home and beautiful interior presentations. From 1341' to 3775'. $4.95

5) Photographed Portraits of an American Home™
100 of our finest designs, beautifully photographed and tastefully presented among charming photo album memories of "home." A must for any sales center's coffee table. $14.95

6) Gold Seal™ Home Plan Book Set – 442 of today's most sought-after one-story, 1 1/2 story and 2-story home plan ideas. All 5 books for $84.95 or $19.95 each

- Homes of Distinction – 86 plans under 1800'
- Homes of Sophistication – 106 plans, 1800'-2199'
- Homes of Elegance – 107 plans, 2200'-2599'
- Homes of Prominence – 75 plans, 2600'-2999'
- Homes of Grandeur – 68 plans, 3000'-4000'

7) Timeless Legacy™, A Collection of Fine Home Designs by Carmichael & Dame – 52 breathtaking luxury home designs from 3300' to 4500'. Includes artful rear views of each home. $25.00

8) The Homes of Carmichael & Dame™ Vol. II
60 elegant designs from simple to sublime. From 1751' to 4228'. $9.95

9) *Seasons of Life™
Designs for Reaping the Rewards of Autumn
100 home plans specially tailored to today's empty-nester. From 1212' to 3904'. $4.95

10) *Seasons of Life™
Designs for Living Summer's Journey – 100 designs for the move-up buyer. From 1605' to 3775'. $4.95

11) *Seasons of Life™
Designs for Spring's New Beginnings – 100 home plans for first-time buyers. Presentations unique to this lifestyle. From 1125' to 2537'. $4.95

12) W.L. Martin Home Designs™
53 beautiful home plans offering outstanding livability. From 1262' to 3914'. $9.95

13) The Narrow Home Plan™ Collection
258 one-story, 1 1/2 story and 2-story home plans that are from 26 to 50 feet wide. This book also includes 25 duplex plans. $14.95

14) Nostalgia Home Plans Collection™
A New Approach to Time-Honored Design
70 designs showcasing enchanting details and unique "special places." From 1339' to 3480'. $9.95

15) Nostalgia Home Plans Collection™ Vol. II
A New Approach to Time-Honored Design
70 designs bringing back the essence of homes of the past. $9.95

16) Gold Seal Favorites™ – 100 best selling plans from the famous Gold Seal™ Collection, including 25 duplex designs. $6.95

17) Easy Living One-Story Designs™
155 one-story home designs from the Gold Seal™, Heartland Home Plans™ and Timeless Legacy™ collections, together in one plan book. $7.95

*Order the complete Seasons of Life™ set (all three books) for only $9.00

15.

14.

258

THE NARROW HOME PLAN COLLECTION

13.

W.L. MARTIN HOME DESIGNS

12.

3. HEARTLAND HOME PLANS™
Designs with a New Appreciation for Traditional American Values

4. Reflections American Home

5. Photographed Portraits American Home

6.

ORDER DIRECT
TOLL-FREE
(800) 947~7526
www.designbasics.com

8.

7.

11. SEASONS OF LIFE

SEASONS OF LIFE

SEASONS OF LIFE

10.

9.

9R

A PLAN FROM CARMICHAEL & DAME: WHAT'S IN IT FOR YOU?

Plans come to you on high-quality reproducible vellums and include the following:

Cover Page Each Carmichael & Dame home plan features the rendered elevation and informative reference sections including: general notes and design criteria;* abbreviations; and symbols for your Carmichael & Dame plan.

Elevations Drafted at ¼" scale for the front and ⅛" scale for the rear and sides. All elevations are detailed and an aerial view of the roof is provided, showing all hips, valleys and ridges.

Foundations Drafted at ¼" scale. Block foundations and basements are standard. We also show the HVAC equipment, structural information,* steel beam and pole locations and the direction and spacing of the floor system above.

Main Level Floor Plan ¼" scale. Fully dimensioned from stud to stud for ease of framing. 2"x4" walls are standard. The detailed drawings include such things as structural header locations, joist sizes and spacings.

Second Level Floor Plan ¼" scale. Dimensioned from stud to stud and drafted to the same degree of detail as the main level floor plan.*

Interior Elevations Useful for the cabinet and bidding process, this page shows all kitchen and bathroom cabinets as well as any other cabinet elevations.

Electrical and Sections Illustrated on a separate page for clarity, the electrical plan shows suggested electrical layout for the foundation, main and second level floor plans. Typical wall, cantilever, stair, brick and fireplace sections are provided to further explain construction of these areas.

All plan orders received prior to 2:00 p.m. CT will be processed, inspected and shipped out same afternoon via 2nd business day air within the continental United States. All other prod orders will be sent via UPS ground service. Full Technical Support is available for any plan p chase from Carmichael & Dame. Our Technical Support Specialists provide unlimited techni support free of charge and answer questions regarding construction methods, framing te niques and more. Please call 800-947-7526 for more information.

CONSTRUCTION LICENSE

When you purchase a Carmichael & Dame home plan, you receive a Construction Licer which gives you certain rights in building the home depicted in that plan, including:

No Re-Use Fee. As the original purchaser of a Carmichael & Dame home plan, Construction License permits you to build the plan as many times as you like.

Local Modifications. The Construction License allows you to make modifications to yo Carmichael & Dame plans. We offer a complete custom change service, or you may ha the desired changes done locally by a qualified draftsman, designer, architect or engineer

Running Blueprints. If your plans are sent to you on vellum paper they will reprodu well on your blueprint machine. The Construction License authorizes you or your bluepr facility, at your direction, to make as many copies of the plan from the vellum masters you need for construction purposes.

*Carmichael & Dame cannot warrant compliance with any specific code or regulation because codes and requirements may vary from jurisdiction to jurisdiction. Consult your local building official to determine the suitability of these plans for your specific site and appli tion. This plan was also designed in seismic zone 1. This plan can be adapted to your local building codes and requirements, but also, it is the responsibility of the purchaser and/or builder of this plan to see that the structure is built in strict compliance with all governm municipal codes (city, county, state and federal).

TO ORDER DIRECT: CALL 800-947-7526 • MONDAY – FRIDAY 7:00 a.m. – 6:00 p.m. CT

Name _____   Company _____

Address _____   Title _____

(For UPS Delivery – Packages cannot be shipped to a P.O. Box.)

Above Address: ☐ business address ☐ residence address

City _____ State _____ Zip _____

☐ VISA [VISA]   ☐ MasterCard [MasterCard]   Credit Card: [ ][ ][ ][ ][ ][ ][ ][ ][ ][ ][ ][ ][ ][ ][ ][ ]

Phone ( ) _____ FAX ( ) _____

We appreciate it when you use VISA or MasterCard.

Expiration Date: [ ][ ] / [ ][ ]

☐ Check enclosed ☐ AMEX ☐ Discover

Signature _____

✓	HOME PLAN PRODUCTS	PLAN #	QTY.	PRICE	SHIPPING & HANDLING	TOTAL
☐	1 Set of Master Vellum Prints or 5 Sets of Blueprints					$
☐	Add'l. Sets of Blueprints - $40.00					$
☐	Materials List - $50.00 (if available)					$
☐	Study Print & Furniture Layout Guide™ - $29.95 (if available)					$
☐	Specifications & Finishing Checklist™ - $14.95					$
☐						$
BOOK NUMBER	**BOOK NAME**					
☐	Complete Plan Book Library – $150.00					$
						$
						$

• CALL FOR • Shipping & Handling Charges

• No COD Orders • US Funds Only •
NO REFUNDS OR EXCHANGES, PLEASE

CALL 800-947-7526
OR MAIL ORDER TO: **Design Basics**
11112 John Galt Blvd.
Omaha, NE 68137

PRICES SUBJECT TO CHANGE

Subtotal $

TX Residents Add 6.25% Tax
NE Residents Add 6.5% Tax $

Total $

PLAN PRICE SCHEDULE

Plan Price Code	Total Sq. Ft.	Plan Price
17	1700' - 1799'	$570
18	1800' - 1899'	$580
19	1900' - 1999'	$590
20	2000' - 2099'	$600
21	2100' - 2199'	$610
22	2200' - 2299'	$620
23	2300' - 2399'	$630
24	2400' - 2499'	$640
25	2500' - 2599'	$650
26	2600' - 2699'	$660
27	2700' - 2799'	$670
28	2800' - 2899'	$680
29	2900' - 2999'	$690
30	3000' - 3099'	$700
31	3100' - 3199'	$710
32	3200' - 3299'	$720
33	3300' - 3399'	$730
34	3400' - 3499'	$740
35	3500' - 3599'	$750
36	3600' - 3699'	$760
37	3700' - 3799'	$770
38	3800' - 3899'	$780
39	3900' - 3999'	$790
40	4000' - 4099'	$800
41	4100' - 4199'	$810
42	4200' - 4299'	$820
43	4300' - 4399'	$830
44	4400' - 4499'	$840
45	4500' - 4599'	$850